CONTENTS

5

PART 1

THE POWER OF THE PURR

Our feline pets enrich our lives and
radiate a sense of balance, connectivity and calm.

When your kitty stares at you and slowly blinks, consider it a sign of great affection.

IRRESISTIBLE

CUTEST CATS

With their big eyes, small noses and large foreheads, cats resemble adorable human babies.

If your indoor cat regularly goes outside, make sure he is up to date on his vaccinations.

Enchanting and delightfully calm, Ragdoll cats stay attuned to your feelings and moods.

Gray cats and orange tabbies get adopted at the highest rates.

U.S. shelters are overflowing with adorable mixed-breed kittens available for adoption.

Kittens trigger a deep response in the human brain, tapping into the same impulse that compels us to care for our own young.

Kittens should ideally stay with their littermates for their first 12 weeks.

Spirited and playful, kittens love exploring the natural world and running free outdoors.

Playtime helps kittens increase coordination and social skills.

A cat's wide-open pupils indicate excitement or fear; narrow ones can mean anger.

Human love can provide a sense of total safety for cats, animals who are skittish in the wild.

FOR THE LOVE OF CATS

Our affection for our felines is often over-the-top.
Here's why we feel such deep emotion for them.

Owning a cat can
help teach children
about empathy.

The Siamese
cat, shown here,
is chatty and
seductive.

As the internet was picking up steam in the early aughts, we had our choice of animals, ideas and movie icons to share far and wide. But the most enduring meme turned out to be the cat. First there was the newsgroup rec.pets.cats, where folks posted photos of their felines with abandon. In 2006, the funny-looking "lolcat" started making the rounds with an associated website, "I Can Has Cheezburger?" (supposedly the words of lolcat itself). People went wild. Soon we had Keyboard Cat, Grumpy Cat and Lil Bub. When the media juggernaut Buzzfeed launched in 2006, its cat images went viral worldwide.

The burning question remains: Why cats? Why do we have such outsized love for the felines who are now our family members and sharing our homes?

BABY-FACED

One clear answer is that, with their big eyes, small noses and mouths, bulging cheeks and large foreheads, cats closely resemble a human baby—a seductive, irresistible call for love to any human mind. It was the ethologist Konrad Lorenz who first pointed out that we become attached to human infants through this specific configuration of facial features.

Now, research into the phenomenon extends to our pets, especially cats. One compelling study comes from John Archer, a professor of psychology at the University of Central Lancashire in the United Kingdom. Archer found that women, especially, are drawn to pets with infantile features. And people who said they were especially close to their cats ranked highest in this attraction.

> Your cat likes to mark you. When you take on the scent of your cat's pheromones, you start to feel like family.

Rubbing up against you is a sign your cat loves you.

Still more evidence comes from Marta Borgi and Francesca Cirulli, researchers at the Istituto Superiore di Sanità in Rome. In their study of children aged 3 to 6, they found a preference for more infantile cats, especially kittens. The children ranked infantile features in kitties more favorably than infantile features in dogs, where they did not prefer puppies over adult dogs.

Adding to the effect, of course, is the persistent, high-pitched meow, like a baby's cry—a siren call of love and need to the human brain. Cats perfected this call for help over millennia of domestication—even tailoring specific rhythms and accents to humans in the home.

LOVE TOTEMS

A cat's infantile appearance, while alluring, is hardly the only reason these pets garner our love. Their ability to literally receive our love makes us adore them more. According to John Bradshaw, foundation director of the Anthrozoology Institute at the University of Bristol in England and author of *Cat Sense* and *The Animals Among Us: How Pets Make Us Human*, cats can literally light up our brain. Physical contact with our kitties, he notes, can produce changes in levels of the attachment hormone oxytocin. "Within the brain," he writes in *The Animals Among Us*, "nerves with oxytocin receptors make contact with several areas important for memory and feelings of reward and emotion." Just stroking your cat can stimulate the oxytocin pathway, eliciting feelings of closeness and love.

And don't forget the cats' purr. At a frequency of 26 to 140 hertz, the purr falls into the range doctors use to help regenerate tissue. Among other benefits, the vibratory sound lowers human stress—and, say studies, can reduce the occurrence of heart attacks by some 40 percent.

All this amounts to something like love. But the best testimony comes from cat owners themselves.

"My cat has a daily bedtime routine with me and

A purring cat is happy and content. When a cat feels safe, he can start to relax.

Some research shows cats have stronger bonds with women than men.

19

While your cat plays at home, she is also looking up to make sure you're watching, and still around.

Cats need attention too! Spend some time each day engaging with them.

sleeps by my pillow. I can feel her strong personality next to me. It's like I'm her mom," says Rebekah Gillette of New Hampshire.

"Throughout my life, my kitties have entertained me, loved me, snuggled with me. Their purr helps me fall asleep, they welcome me when I get home. They make sure I get out of bed. They give me an excuse to stay in bed! They're amazingly smart and know when I need extra attention. They calm me with their soft fur and they're not nearly as slick as they think they are (talking about you Dave, Leo and Soxy). They enrich my life," notes Jenni Barnett of California.

"My cat keeps me in line," adds Traci Brehm of Florida. He "pulls my hair until I get up at 5:30 a.m. to feed him, sits on the tub while I take a bath—I assume to make sure I don't drown—and falls asleep on me at bedtime, I guess to make sure that I don't fall out of bed." 🐾

Time spent bonding with your cat benefits you both.

YOUR REWARD

THE CAT ADVANTAGE

A host of research shows that living with kitties can boost your mood, enhance your health and even improve your love life.

Cat (and dog) owners score higher than nonowners on measures of sensitivity and trust.

Cats aren't just adorable, pleasing to the eye and lovely to touch. They also bring very real benefits to human well-being, lifting mood, lowering risk of heart disease and stroke and, believe it or not, even easing our allergies.

Here are 10 perks to spending time with cats that may come as a surprise:

1 Lower Stress

Having a cat can stimulate production of the love and bonding hormone, oxytocin, making you calmer, less lonely and less stressed.

2 Reduce the Risk of Heart Attack

Just petting your cat can calm you down, but doctors speculate this soothing effect may reduce your risk of cardiovascular disease. "Acquisition of cats as domestic pets may represent a novel strategy for reducing the risk of cardiovascular diseases in high-risk individuals," according to a study from the University of Minnesota. The researchers found that cat owners were at least 30 percent less likely to die of a heart attack or stroke than nonowners, though some speculate that a person who loves cats may be naturally calmer to begin with.

If you own a cat, make sure you mention that on your dating app profile for optimum success!

Research has shown that those who own cats are especially open to new experiences.

3 Help Heal Injuries

Your kitty's purrs range between 25 and 140 Hz, the wavelength frequency also shown to aid the repair of bones, joints and tendons, and the healing of wounds. Researchers point out that cats recover quickly from these injuries and purrs may be at the root.

4 Ease Headaches

Anecdotally, some people report that their migraines clear more rapidly when lying or cuddling with their furry friend.

5 Help With Sleep

Studies show that more than half of those who own cats actually sleep with them between the sheets, with good reason. Researchers say that just having your cat in bed reduces anxiety and night terrors.

6 Reduce Allergies

Cats are notorious for causing allergic reactions due to the their dandruff-like flakes known as dander. But now, a study from the National Institute of Allergy and Infectious Diseases shows that children raised with two or more dogs or cats during the first year of life may be less likely to develop an allergy compared with children raised without pets. "Pet exposure early in life appears to protect against not only pet allergy but also other types of common allergies, such as allergy to dust mites, ragweed and grass," says allergist Marshall Plaut, MD.

7 Can Look After Your Health and Even Save Your Life

Yes, your cat *can* be that into you. One cat we know helped her owner turn off a CPAP sleep apnea device each morning. Another feline warned her human of impending epileptic seizures, and a Montana couple were alerted by their cat to a gas leak.

8 Owning a Cat Will Help Men Get Dates

A recent study reports that 90 percent of single women rated men as nicer if they happened to own a cat versus guys who didn't have a feline friend.

9 Even YouTube Cats Are a Positive

The phenomenon of watching funny cat videos on the internet boosts viewers' energy and

Scientists say cats are more in tune with human emotions than we once thought.

positive emotions and decreases negative feelings, according to a study from The Media School at Indiana University.

10 Reduce Your Carbon Footprint (Compared to a Dog)

Dogs eat so much meat that owning one is equivalent to driving an SUV. Cats consume less and have been compared to driving a little Hyundai. ❦

Preying on Your Mind

IT'S NO SECRET THAT A CAT RUNNING free outdoors can be the holy terror of the neighborhood, stalking, hunting and killing small birds along with mice and other mammals. Now, a study published in January 2019 by the British Ecological Society reveals that many cat owners are indeed disturbed when their well-fed cats kill other animals outdoors. "The growing cat population may place more pressure on vulnerable species," researchers from the University of Exeter say. Many of those interviewed were conflicted because they felt their cats needed outdoor time for a full life, yet worried about the pain inflicted on other innocent creatures when their cats ran free. Some were especially disturbed when their pets brought trophy prey inside their homes for sport. The researchers urge owners to take responsibility for their cats outdoors and say that enrichment at home through toys and play may help to curb predatory hunting outdoors.

Cats don't lose their hunting instinct.

27

THE HAPPY CAT

Our cats make us happy, but how can we know if we are returning the gift?
Samantha Bell, cat behavior and enrichment lead for Best Friends Animal Society
in Los Angeles, believes cats let us know how they're feeling through a series
of signs and tells. Here, she offers advice on how to make sure your cat is content.

How can we tell when our cats are happy?

A happy cat is a confident cat, with tail held high and a relaxed body and face. When a cat walks toward you with his tail up and quivering, he's bursting with happiness and excitement. When a cat is lying near you and purring, she's relaxed and content. Being a prey species, cats demonstrate that they feel safe and happy with us by showing their vulnerable side. When they relax, close their eyes or expose their tummy, they're telling us they feel safe with us and don't need to be on the lookout for danger or stressors.

What other signs should we look for?

Chirping, playfulness, head-butting, kneading, having a good appetite, grooming themselves and you, and slow-blinking at you are all good signs that you have a happy cat.

Can you explain head-butting and kneading?

When a cat bumps her head into you, she's saying she's your friend, that she trusts you by placing her head so close to you.

Even from a young age cats enjoy making physical contact.

Cats knead you with their paws when they're content. Some say it's because they associate this motion with the comforts of nursing on their mama, their first happy memory.

How can we tell if our cats are happy to see us?

Maybe they just want to be fed. It's a little bit of both. Being fed brings happiness to most cats. And if we are the ones that bring the food, then we are making them happy.

Why is rubbing up against us a happy sign?

It's a greeting and a sign of affection. Cats live scent-based lives, and they want to create and maintain a 'family scent' with the humans and cats they like. They rub the parts of their body that are full of their own pheromones on you to try to make you smell like family. 🐾

When a cat is feeling relaxed, she'll often close her eyes.

YOUR CAT ADORES YOU

Seeing the world through your
pet's eyes requires an intuitive mentality.

Dog people are always telling cat people that dogs care more about humans than cats do. But now, recent research from Oregon State University reveals that in addition to cats enjoying our company, they may even choose us over food. To do the research, investigators including Kristyn Shreve, Lindsay Mehrkam and Monique Udell deprived 50 cats, including pets and shelter animals, of human interaction, food, toys and scents for a few hours. Then they tempted the animals with a few varieties of each of those same stimuli. For example, the scent offerings included catnip, gerbil and the odor of a strange cat; researchers rated the preference based on which smells (or foods) the feline interacted with for the longest period of time. Although there was clear individual variability in cat preference, social interaction with humans was the most-preferred stimulus category for the majority of cats after the hourslong break. Food wound up in second place.

"It is still common belief that cats are not especially sociable or trainable," the authors say. But a more complex picture has begun to emerge. We've long known that cats can be conditioned to engage in numerous behaviors using straightforward behavioral training. And now, research has revealed increasingly complex social, cognitive and problem-solving abilities in our feline friends.

How to reconcile our beliefs with the reality? The study from Shreve and team does just that. It could be that all along, we've been confused about the stimuli cats really prefer (us), making the motivation we give them to step up to the plate and learn what we want absolutely subpar. Indeed, a whole industry has evolved around training our cats with wands, clickers and special, tasty treats. But what if the best reward for a job well done is just more time with the human of choice? In the future, we can use this newfound preference for humans to successfully motivate cats in training programs and in our homes. 🐾

Cats enjoy the company
of humans just as much
as their alone time.

Cats are considered to be members of the family by 99 percent of their owners.

Give 'em treats!

MAKE YOUR CAT LOVE YOU

Easy ways to strengthen your bond.

Treat your cat like an independent agent.
Sure, you've got to take care of her, but remember that your cat is not a dog; a cat needs space to go off on her own. She may enjoy it when you pet her, but her taste for interaction with people has its limits. Don't hold her endlessly on your lap, and when she retreats to a far corner of the room to hide, just let her be.

Avoid making sustained eye contact with your cat.
Cats see this kind of staring as a threat—instead, when you look at your cat, make sure to blink at him.

Engage in play with your cat.
Purchase a few simple toys; try attaching one to a string so that the cat perceives it as prey. You can make toys fly like birds or scamper like mice. Your cat will love pouncing on toys moving in front of him.

Motivate your cat through treats, not punishment.
If you try to discipline your cat through yelling or aggression, he will just run out of the room and away from you. Instead, find the food he likes best and give him a piece whenever he does something well. Go for small, healthy treats that won't increase his risk of obesity; try small bites of chicken or tuna.

Brush your cat's fur.
Not only is this grooming healthy for skin and fur, cats love it. But here's a tip: Use long, gentle strokes and avoid brushing against the fur's grain, which could cause discomfort. ❀

FAMILY

WHY CATS RESEMBLE THEIR OWNERS

Do you and Fluffy share more than a few features?

Dogs famously bear an uncanny resemblance to their owners, but the phenomenon isn't limited to man's best friend. Felines also take after their human counterparts—or perhaps it's the other way around. Cat owners tend to be more introverted, neurotic, spontaneous and unconventional than dog owners—qualities that also describe most cats. According to animal behaviorist Stanley Coren, people who own cats are more apt to live on their own in an apartment and tend to be exclusively devoted to them. We like what we like, including less responsibility and more freedom—another trait we share with our feline familiars. Like when people choose friends and mates, we gravitate toward cats who share our characteristics—the runt of the litter, the goofball, the sleepyhead, the troublemaker.

Twenty percent of pet owners report shared personality traits, and for those who have owned their pets for more than seven years, that number jumps to 40 percent. Psychologist Richard Wiseman says this phenomenon happens in humans as well: "Married couples...grow to look like each other and to have similar personalities. It's possible we are seeing a similar effect [with cats and their owners]." If

We gravitate to cats who share our characteristics, be it a glamour-puss or the runt of the litter.

I'm affectionate or playful, my cat is more likely to be that way too, especially if I get her as a kitten. A *Journal of Veterinary Behavior* study found that indoor cats "mirrored the lives of their owners," while outdoor cats tend to adopt the habits of neighborhood felines.

Cats are affected by nurture as well as nature, adapting to human routines around eating, sleeping and using the bathroom. Cats with litter boxes in the bathroom frequently use them when their owners are on the toilet. I often wonder what my cat is thinking when she does this—is she mirroring my behavior, or does she find it funny? Perhaps she's oblivious, but I don't think so.

As with human-human relationships, cats also influence their owners. Notably, cats seem to believe humans are big cats. Cat-behavior expert John Bradshaw believes "cats behave toward us in a way that's indistinguishable from [how] they act toward other cats." Cats lick us, sniff us and rub our legs. Many owners have no problem acting the part—I stretch out in the sunny spot on the floor and chase my cat on all fours, though I draw the line at eating her food. Ultimately, it's unclear who trains whom in these relationships. We might think we call the shots, but cats descended from royalty—and they won't let us forget it. —*Joelle Renstrom* 🐾

Cats naturally adapt to our own behaviors and routines.

35

PART 2

HISTORY OF CATS

Cats lived among the first human farmers, inhabited the palaces of Egypt and traveled worldwide by ship.

IN THE COMPANY OF CATS

How cats have survived, thrived and captivated us for thousands of years.

I f your cat's bossy attitude and entertaining antics have you catering to her needs, you are not alone. Your thoroughly modern kitty is descended from a long line of ancestors who likely used those same skills to cajole, sneak and work their way into the lives of humans for thousands of years.

"What sort of philosophers are we, who know absolutely nothing about the origin and destiny of cats?" the American essayist, naturalist and feline lover Henry David Thoreau asked back in the 19th century. Today, the answers are finally at hand: Thanks to new archaeological discoveries and advances in DNA analysis, we've come up with some surprising insights into this most ancient pet.

DOWN ON THE FARM

DNA studies have traced most of today's domesticated cats, species name Felis silvestris catus, to ancient wildcats of the subspecies Felis silvestris lybica. These wildcats were found in North Africa and the Near East at the dawn of human farming some 10,000 years ago, and genetic analysis shows that most cats had the stripes and coloring we associate with today's tabby.

> Cats working on farms some 10,000 years ago, at the dawn of human agriculture, looked like the tabbies of today.

Feline ancestors of today's domestic cats still live and thrive in Asia and Africa.

A Southern African wildcat (Felis lybica cafra), perches in a tree.

This cat mummy dates to between 672 B.C. and 332 B.C. and sits in the Louvre.

Archaeological evidence concurs: Stone and clay statues up to 10,000 years old suggest that cats were culturally important in the areas that are now Syria, Turkey and Israel. And bones of cats from about that time period have also been found on the island of Cyprus, where they presumably arrived by boat.

There's evidence that at least some of the cats could have been pets at that time, too. Jean-Denis Vigne, head researcher at the French National Centre for Scientific Research, and colleagues discovered the remains of a cat on Cyprus, buried close to a 9,500-year-old human grave filled with valuables like polished stones. The cat and man, in similar states of preservation, were both positioned with heads pointed west. That suggests to Vigne that the cat could well have been a beloved pet.

GLORY DAYS IN EGYPT

Researchers say that cats have long been helpers to human farmers in several areas of the Mediterranean and the Near East. But some 4,000 years ago, in ancient Egypt, they were elevated in status to much, much more. "Egypt was an agrarian society, and therefore cats became very important to the people who were tilling the fields and storing the grain, because cats could get rid of vermin. But it didn't take long for cats to find their way into Egyptian homes and then become part of the ancient Egyptians' everyday routine," explains Egyptologist Melinda Hartwig. "But Egyptians didn't domesticate cats. Cats domesticated themselves. They were lovable pets as well as hunters."

The ancient Egyptians looked at the natural world and saw in it the embodiment of the divine, Hartwig, curator of Egyptian art at Emory University's Michael C. Carlos Museum, explains. "They didn't look at cats as divine, but they saw cats as having a spark of what makes divinity."

From that came depictions of gods and goddesses with feline qualities, often animal heads and human bodies. Two of the most important cat goddesses in Egyptian mythology were the fierce lion-headed goddess Sekhmet, a protector of justice, and Bastet, associated with the home, fertility and childbirth.

> In ancient Egyptian mythology Bastet was a cat goddess of fertility, childbirth and home.

Ancient Egyptians looked at cats and saw in them the spark of divinity.

A bronze statuette of Bastet, a sacred animal to the Egyptians.

41

A visit to *Divine Felines: Cats of Ancient Egypt*, an exhibition at the Carlos Museum, reveals the pervasiveness of cats in Egyptian life: cat-shaped wooden coffins for cat mummies; amulets in cat forms; luxury items decorated with felines; and a cast-bronze figurine of a cat nursing four kittens. Tomb paintings show cats, realistically portrayed, peering out from under their masters' chairs.

Notably, when felines died, they were embalmed, mummified and buried with or near their owners; living, grieving humans shaved off their own eyebrows in mourning when their pet cats expired. Statues of cats were often adorned with gold earrings and nose rings. Were Egyptians so taken with their feline companions that they made jewelry for them?

"That's the main question I get asked at lectures," Hartwig answers with a laugh. "My answer, always, is this—would you want to pierce a cat's ear? You'd be sliced and diced. Most likely, the addition of jewelry on the statues was to show that cats were an aspect of the sun god Ra. The gold jewelry is yellow, like the sun."

BRUTALITY OF THE CAT INQUISITION

At first, reverence for cats spread around the globe. Cats in Norse and Celtic myths from Europe, for instance, are depicted as magical and powerful. But it was not to last. With the rise of the Roman Empire and the Christian church more than 2,000 years ago, pagan symbols—including those of cats—were widely rejected.

Felines were attacked and slaughtered across Europe, especially after Pope Gregory IX (1227–1241) launched the Inquisition. He denounced cats as so evil as to be in league with Satan. That's when the image of the witch with the black cat took hold in the popular mind.

CATS RISE AGAIN

But due to their survival skills in the wild—and, no doubt, to humans who sheltered cats from the feline version of the Inquisition—cats persisted. As settlers traveled around the world on ships, they took their cats with them. These cats kept vermin aboard ocean vessels under control, and they became pets and helpers for farmers and other humans on land.

The cat's route from the hot, desert climes of the Middle East through Europe to the Americas was via long journeys by sea. "Though cats are said to hate water, it has always been their way around," writes Abigail Tucker in *The Lion in the Living Room*. As companions on ships, cats not only kept the rat population down during the long voyages, Tucker points out, but they were particularly suited to ocean journeys: Coming from the desert, they didn't need much water. And, unlike humans, they didn't even

Street cats have been prowling about for thousands of years.

need vitamin C, so scurvy in cats was not an issue at all. Plus, perhaps most importantly, the cats kept travelers company.

Tucker says that mariners have long invented cat toys, and "over the centuries, cats became such a quintessential part of ship culture that many superstitious old salts wouldn't come aboard unless cats were also conscripted." And so, cat companions spread worldwide.

> Cats have been transformed over thousands of years from wild animals to members of the family.

DOMESTIC TECH BRINGS KITTY HOME

The elevation of the cat to cherished family member, not just for royalty but for the masses, made its final climb over the past 75 years. That massive shift in how cats live was aided by crucial advancements in technology. Our human interventions—including new and improved kitty litter that allowed cats to relieve themselves indoors, better cat nutrition, and advanced scientific methods of birth control—allowed the once-wild animals called cats to bridge the gap to domesticity, and today, live entirely indoors with us. 🐾

On ships, cats can keep rats under control.

Cats explored new lands with their human settlers.

FROM ASHES TO AWESOME

THE STORY OF CAT LITTER

How a simple invention changed the way our two species interact.

Modern kitty litter has allowed cats to live inside.

Cats were largely relegated to the outdoors until the arrival of a 20th-century concept: the indoor "toilet" equivalent for felines, the litter box, allowing cats to be domesticated at last. Messy and sometimes unsanitary things like ashes, dirt, sawdust and sand were first used in boxes so that cats who lived inside could "do their business." But the lives of cats and cat owners changed dramatically in 1948, when a Michigan man named Edward Lowe gave us modern litter.

Lowe worked in his father's company, which sold industrial absorbents like sawdust and clay. One day a neighbor asked if he had any extra sawdust. She'd been using ashes in a box for her cat to "go" in, which left paw prints all over her home. Lowe had a bag of liquid-absorbent clay called fuller's earth handy, and he thought that might work better.

It did. The neighbor noted that the clay didn't track, and vowed never again to use anything else in her feline's box. She shared the news with cat-loving neighbors, and demand for the clay grew.

The rest was a new chapter in cat history. Absorbent litter, which cut down on the strong odor of cat urine as well as the tracking problem, likely played a large role in the popularity of pet cats.

Over the years, a host of different types of cat litters have been developed. Some are made from recycled newspaper and even corn, but most still rely on some form of clay.

Most modern litters often include many additives that Lowe's original Kitty Litter never contained, like clumping agents; anti-dust sprays, including PTFE (better known as Teflon); and perfume-like scents.

Litter boxes themselves now come in a large variety, too—deep pans, covered boxes and disposable pans. Battery-powered self-cleaning litter boxes work with a rake-like instrument that moves across and through the litter, sifting out waste and depositing it into a receptacle at one end of the box that closes automatically. This holds in odors until the cat owner removes and dumps the container.

But are these improvements always best for cats? And do cats even like them?

Cats seem most agreeable to a clumping, unscented, simple litter, according to Atlanta veterinarian Tabitha Tanis, DVM. She notes that opting for low-dust, unscented litter is especially important for cats; moreover, they often dislike the feeling of different-shaped pellets and the crystals found in "fancier" litters.

"If your cat is not scratching in their litter and covering their waste, they may not like the way the litter feels," Tanis says.

When it comes to litter boxes, meanwhile, shallow, open pans are often preferred by cats, especially elderly felines with arthritis, although some will adjust to boxes with closed tops. ☙

Kittens have a natural instinct to eliminate in sand or soil.

SAFER SPAYING AND NEUTERING

Understanding the benefits of these now-routine procedures.

Cats' sex lives were long a problem for humans. When feline reproductive systems were unchecked, females went into heat, "calling for mates" and producing litters of mostly unwanted kittens. Male cats roamed, looking for females, and fought loudly with each other, causing injuries and infections. So it's no wonder some cat lovers turned to spaying females and neutering males when it was first offered in the 19th century. However, back then it was anything but easy on the pets.

In the 1893 pamphlet *The Diseases of Dogs and Cats and Their Treatment*, an anonymous veterinarian described rolling male cats up tightly in blankets so their legs were immobilized as the vet castrated them, usually with no anesthesia (unless pet owners paid extra for chloroform). Another described an approach to neutering a male cat that involved sticking the animal's head in a boot and castrating them with a knife while the tomcat's rear was stuck in the air.

"Female castration" was available, too, and involved two incisions to remove the ovaries. By 1925, veterinarian Hamilton Kirk described advances in spaying and neutering—including using anesthesia and sterilizing surgical instruments—in his book *The Diseases of the Cat and Its General Management*.

Although spaying and neutering cats became more widely available in the 1930s, the feral, stray and unwanted cat population dumped at shelters increased. Before 1970, euthanasia rates in the U.S. rapidly increased—and shelters routinely euthanized more than 100 cats (and dogs) per 1,000 people in their communities, according to the Humane Society of the United States.

With the advent of low-cost spay-and-neuter facilities in the late 20th century and the accumulation of evidence showing that neutering procedures weren't cruel but helpful to cats, most pet owners came to agree that having their kitties "fixed" was a responsible and necessary part of pet ownership.

Ovariohysterectomy, which removes the ovaries, fallopian tubes and uterus from a female cat, and orchiectomy, which removes the testes from a male cat, are the most popular forms of neutering cats today. The health benefits of these surgical procedures include reducing the risk of uterine infections and breast cancer in females, and lessening the risk of testicular cancer in males. Fears that neutering and spaying would affect a cat's intelligence or ability to play are now known to be unfounded. What's more, reducing cats' breeding instinct makes them less inclined to roam, and more content to be stay-at-home pets. ∎

Cats live longer, healthier lives if they don't give birth to litter after litter.

FROM RATS AND TABLE SCRAPS TO GOURMET DISHES

Tracing the path to the modern supper dish.

Long before anything known as "cat food"—made specifically for felines—was invented, cats were taking care of their own high-protein nutrition needs, catching mice, birds and whatever else they found hunting in the wild. Cats lucky enough to live near or with humans were often offered table scraps. But in the latter part of the 19th century, there was a change. While working in London, American lightning-rod salesman James Spratt saw dogs gobbling up leftover biscuits from a ship and was inspired to create the first commercially prepared pet food—initially for dogs, then for cats. The company, Spratt's, was so successful in England that a U.S. operation was opened in 1870.

Cat lover and writer Gordon Stables' 1876 book, *Cats: Their Points and Characteristics* (still in print), urged people to feed cats regularly instead of leaving them to live off of hunting alone. In addition to table scraps, Stables endorsed the then-new food made especially for cats: Spratt's kibble, sold in packets.

By the 1900s, commercial cat food was gaining in popularity and by the 1950s, was widely available in versions including canned, dry and semi-moist. The variety of cat foods—countless shapes and colors, catchy names and new formulations, fortified with nutrients—has continued to grow into the 21st century.

But the well-fed cats of today are, too often, overfed. Like American humans, cats in the U.S. are facing an obesity epidemic. Veterinarians now classify about 60 percent of cats as obese, raising the risk for

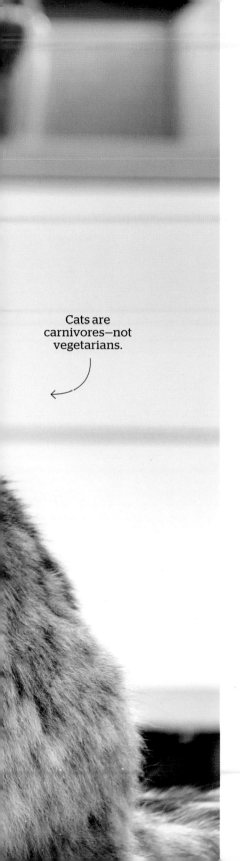

Cats are carnivores—not vegetarians.

feline arthritis, high blood pressure, kidney disease and certain cancers.

Not all cat food may be the healthiest choice for your cat, according to feline-health experts. Talk to your veterinarian about the best kind—and appropriate amount—of food for your cat.

SMART NUTRITION TIPS FOR 21ST-CENTURY CATS

Look for the term "AAFCO Approved" on the label of cat food. The American Association of Feed Control Officers (AAFCO) designation means it meets minimum standards for feline nutrition and ensures a balanced diet, according to cat specialist Drew Weigner, DVM, hospital director of The Cat Doctor, Atlanta's first feline practice.

Not all healthy-sounding cat foods are actually good for cats. "Conventional, organic, grain-free and holistic variations are all available and appropriate for most cats," Weigner points out. "But raw diets, because of their limited shelf life and association with pathogenic bacteria and parasites, are not recommended."

Vegetarianism is fine for people, but not for cats. Felines are obligate carnivores, meaning they rely on nutrients found only in animal sources. Yes, there are vegetarian foods loaded with supplements on the market, but most veterinarians are firmly opposed to no-meat diets for cats. "Cats cannot survive on a vegetarian diet, since they need nutrients that are present only in animal tissue," says Janice Floyd, DVM, director of feline medicine at Briarcliff Animal Clinic in Atlanta. For example, cats need the amino acid taurine for the prevention of eye and heart disease, as well as for reproduction and fetal growth and survival; taurine is found exclusively in foods such as meat and fish.

HOW CAT FOOD CAN TREAT AND HEAL

Starting in the 1970s, veterinarians began selling "prescription" cat foods to help with kidney disease. Advances in nutrition research have increased the use of specific cat foods as medicines. "There is now a plethora of diets available to treat various diseases, from urinary tract stones to intestinal disease and even obesity," says Weigner, who is also president-elect of the nonprofit Winn Feline Foundation, which supports cat-health research.

"More recently," continues Weigner, "diet therapy for diabetic cats has markedly improved quality of life and, in some cases, cured the disease. Considered controversial at the time, research supporting the feline diabetic diet—funded by the Winn Feline Foundation—is now considered foundational, and [it's a] standard therapy for the treatment of diabetic cats." ❖

PART 3

FIND YOUR PERFECT CAT

Discover the breed that you'd like to bring home.

WHAT'S YOUR PEDIGREE?

A consumer's guide to America's most popular cat breeds.

Many people adopt cats that are a happy mix of many types of feline ancestors—black cats can mix with calicos, and short-haired and long-haired parents produce litters as well. But if you decide to get a pedigreed cat, you'll be more likely to have your kitten grow into the cat you envisioned.

WHY GET A BREED?
This is a must for those interested in show cats. But aside from that, buying a breed means you know exactly the kind of animal you are getting—its personality, color, health strengths and weaknesses, and more. And maintaining cat breeds means that these desirable traits will be reliably reproducible, generation in and out. A Siamese is going to be friendly and active, while a Persian will be calmer, quieter and shyer overall. A Maine coon, the size of a small dog, is so hearty that it will play with you into its old age. A Bengal will always look like a small leopard and always love water; a Ragdoll will sit in your lap contentedly—and you can take that to the bank. What's your fancy? To see, here's a rundown of 10 of the most popular breeds in the U.S. ❧

Cats come in all colors, shapes, sizes and personalities!

57

The Siamese is intelligent, lively, friendly and fastidiously clean.

1
Siamese

These beautiful, svelte, short-haired animals with blue eyes and friendly personas were said to come from Thailand, where, according to J. Anne Helgren, the highly regarded author of *The Encyclopedia of Cat Breeds*, they lived in palaces and "served as guardians of precious documents and valuables in the Buddhist temples." They found their way to Britain by the 1800s—and the first Siamese cat in North America inhabited a residence no less elite than the White House, as a gift to Lucy Hayes in 1878. This is a social, vocal and active animal, attuned to human attention and moods.

Best qualities Playful, active and intelligent **Known for** Affection toward owners **Lap cat?** Yes **Weight** 8–15 pounds **Life span** 12–15 years **Cost for a kitten** $400 to $600

You can maintain a Siamese's coat by stroking it with your hands or a silk scarf.

2
Persian

The Persian emerged when short-haired cats mutated for protection against the elements in the cold mountainous regions of Persia (now Iran). It was first brought to Europe in the 17th century by an Italian traveler named Pietro della Valle. By the 1800s, Persians had made it to the United States as well.

Best qualities Playful, yet calm. This cat breed has great affection for owners. **Known for** Compatibility with children and other pets **Lap cat?** Yes **Weight** 9–14 pounds **Life span** 14–15 years **Cost for a kitten** $1,000 to $1,500

The Persian is a longhair with round eyes, full cheeks and ears set widely apart.

3
Maine Coon

The Maine coon is more like a dog than any other cat you can find. It grows to a weight of up to 25 pounds, and it will even wag its tail. At twice the size of the average domestic cat, the Maine Coon will cost twice as much to feed—but for those who love the good health, calm demeanor and friendliness of the breed, it is well worth it. It's only fitting that this cat is named after a state in New England; considered native to North America, it has existed on the American continent since colonial times. The Maine coon neared extinction in the 19th century, as Americans rushed to more exotic arrivals, but today, bolstered by its intelligence, playfulness and good health, it is one of the most popular breeds in the United States.

Best qualities A hearty, robust, sturdy animal that stays healthy for the long haul **Known for** Interacting with your kids. The Maine coon is playful yet calm, affectionate yet independent—this is an intelligent, mellow cat famous for maintaining its activity and disposition into its senior years. **Lap cat?** Yes **Weight** 12–25 pounds **Life span** 12–15 years **Cost for a kitten** between $1,500 and $4,000

The Maine coon is so doglike, it wags its tail. The Ragdoll (right) will love your lap.

4
Ragdoll

While breeds like the Siamese go back thousands of years, the Ragdoll was created in 1964 in Riverside, California, by Ann Baker, a breeder who worked with Persians. Baker created Ragdolls through a neighbor's cat, named Josephine, whose fluffy, long-haired descendents grew large—about 20 pounds, for males. Ragdolls (like the white cat at right) have alluring eyes in shades of ocean blue and are one of the few breeds that love to be held all day long. Not just congenial but downright docile, they literally go limp, like a child's rag doll, when picked up—hence the name. These special cats are intelligent, easygoing and tolerant of many situations and environments. Not only are they fabulous with children, they can actually coexist with dogs. The Ragdoll may be less inclined to hunt than any cat alive, and will instead follow an owner from room to room like a dog. Cat-breed expert Helgren said that Ragdolls are so sweet, "they are devotion wrapped in silky fur, loving loyalty with gentle white paws." They are extremely affectionate, greeting owners at the door. They are also exceptionally relaxed, with "soft polite voices, even at dinnertime." And they love food.

Best qualities Fervent affection toward its owner combined with unending capacity for physical contact with humans **Known for** Robust health and a doglike affect; great with kids **Lap cat?** Yes **Weight** 12–20 pounds **Life span** 12–17 years **Cost for a kitten** $2,000 or more

5
Bengal

This gorgeous cat looks like a jungle feline, complete with leopard's spots. The concept for the breed was launched by crossing an ordinary domestic cat with a leopard cat, an alternate species that resembles a miniature leopard; adult leopard cats are so wild they cannot be tolerated as pets. Researchers thought the mix would be sterile, but one surviving offspring mated with a domestic cat, producing two kittens. Cat historian Helgren notes that one of them was a black cat that inherited a wild, leopard-like temperament. The other was spotted, like the leopard, but with a temperament that was sweet. After many crossings and recrossings, the result was the Bengal, a playful, intelligent ball of fire capable of jumping 4 feet high! Like many domestic cat ancestors, they have affection toward their owners but they're not the best bet for harmonious living with other pets or your kids. When buying a Bengal, do make sure your cat is at least four generations removed from the original leopard cat, or the animal may be difficult to contain.

Best qualities Bengals are balls of fire, active, playful and intelligent **Known for** Athleticism. If you show them affection, they will be loyal companions who return your love **Lap cat?** No **Weight** Male: 10–18 pounds; female: 6–12 pounds **Life span** 12–16 years **Cost for a kitten** $1,500 to $6,000

A Bengal is playful and intelligent. The Himalayan (right) is smart and social.

6
Himalayan

The Himalayan is a cross between a Persian and a Siamese. These round, short-legged felines can't jump far but they are intelligent, mellow and social, making them excellent companions and pets. Due to their long hair, the Himalayan needs constant grooming, so it's a good thing they like being petted by the human who will attend to them each day. This domestic cat is a sweet-tempered companion that embodies some of the best traits of its two ancestral lines.

Best qualities Sweet, playful, smart **Known for** Calmness **Lap cat?** Yes **Life span** 9–15 years **Weight** 7–14 pounds **Cost for a kitten** Between $500 and $1,300

7
American Shorthair

These cats arrived on the American continent with the Europeans and have been here ever since, functioning on farms and in cities as sturdy, working cats charged with killing mice. According to Helgren, these animals are truly a happy medium: your average, all-around cat. They are medium in size and temperament, "the perfect breed for those who want a cat that enjoys being in your lap but not in your face." The independent shorthair does not like being picked up. Its legacy as a worker in our nation's past confers upon it strength, vitality and excellent health. Indeed, this so-called average cat seems average in intelligence, average in affection and average in rambunctiousness—but it excels at being the simple, low-maintenance choice for a family with kids.

Best qualities Friendly but independent, good-natured, sturdy, flexible, healthy **Known for** Being a great all-around pet, a historical legacy as the ultimate worker cat **Lap cat?** Yes **Weight** 6-15 pounds **Life span** 15—20 years **Cost for a kitten:** $600 to $1,200

8
Manx

This round-headed cat with a solid, medium-size body has for centuries been found on the Isle of Man, in the Irish Sea, between Ireland and Britain. Its most famous physical feature could be a lack of a tail, though that doesn't stop it from jumping athletically to the top shelf in a room. This inbred species does have health problems, making the cats especially prone to arthritis, poor eyesight, constipation and spinal deformities. But despite such challenges, the breed's winning personality has kept it at the top of many people's list. These cats are devoted to their humans and enjoy spending time with them. They are playful without being aggressive, making them wonderful pets for families with children or other cats and dogs.

Best qualities Playful without being aggressive, highly social, and quite intelligent **Known for** Seeking time with humans **Lap cat?** Yes **Weight** 7–13 pounds **Life span** 12–14 years **Cost for a kitten** $500 to $1,500

The Manx lacks a tail but is loaded with charm.

Shy Russian Blues tend to favor their own humans and can be wary of strangers.

9
Russian Blue

Cat historians theorize that the breed, with its silver-blue coat and green eyes, came to Britain aboard ships from the White Sea port town of Archangel in northern Russia. These are gentle animals, so reserved that they generally hide when visitors come. They are fastidious and will reject a litter box that is not pristine. They feel unsettled if dinnertime is changed. Despite these quirks, they are affectionate to their own human companions and will follow an owner from room to room, always ready to play. These cats love looking out a window, and they can entertain themselves, but they prefer when their human of choice gets involved.

Best qualities Quiet, calm, sensitive to human moods, truly attached to their owners **Known for** Shyness around strangers **Lap cat?** Yes **Weight** 5–11 pounds **Life span** 10–16 years **Cost for a kitten** About $1,400

The sphynx loves plenty of attention from its humans—and it loves to eat!

The hairless, highly intelligent Sphynx is utterly devoted to its humans.

10
Sphynx

This cat is hairless, making it susceptible to both heat and cold. Hairlessness doesn't make these animals hypoallergenic; like other cats, the sphynx still produces Fel d 1, the protein found in cat saliva and skin secretions that causes some to sneeze and develop headaches and red, itchy eyes. Appearance also doesn't stop people from loving this breed: These exquisitely intelligent animals absolutely love their human companions, demanding attention but returning devotion. They are playful and do fabulously with children. They also eat a lot and require significant work, including a daily bath to cleanse oils off their skin.

Best qualities Loyal, inquisitive, friendly, quiet, gentle **Known for** Stark, hairless appearance and extreme devotion to human owners; playful, affectionate, extremely intelligent **Lap cat?** Yes **Weight** 6–12 pounds **Life span** 12–14 years **Cost for a kitten** From $1,500 to $6,000 ❁

MEANT FOR ME

There's a perfect kitty for everyone.

For Families and Kids

WINNER Birman

The Birman, aka the Sacred Cat of Burma, is renowned for its deep-blue eyes and pure-white "socks" on its paws. It has a long, silky coat that's easy to keep well-groomed, and an inquisitive, affectionate nature that's perfect for kids. Legends abound about the Birman's origins; some say they were ancient Buddhist temple cats, eventually gifted to Europe in the 1900s. Today, Birmans thrive as both house pets and European competition cats.

▼ **RUNNER-UP Chantilly-Tiffany**

Playful, affectionate and extroverted thanks to its combined lineage from longhair cats and Burmese, Tiffanies make perfect family pets.

Birman females mature early, begin "calling" at a young age, and make excellent mothers.

For People With Cat Allergies

WINNER Oriental Shorthair
The Oriental Shorthair boom took place in the 1960s, when Western cat breeders began mating Siamese cats with indigenous breeds, like the British and American Shorthairs. Their short, fine coat and minimal shedding makes them easy to groom and a perfect choice for those with allergies. This breed has the body shape of its Siamese forerunners, but boasts the full-coat color pattern of British and American Shorthairs. They are intelligent, affectionate, dog-like extroverts, who love to be played with, hate to be left alone and often run to greet their owners at the door. Oriental Shorthairs are social cats who prefer to live in pairs or groups.

▼ RUNNER-UP Siberian
Allergen levels produced by mature Siberians are especially low compared to most other breeds, according to a study from the nonprofit Siberian Research, Inc.

Despite their slight appearance, Oriental Shorthairs can leap to high places.

Bombay cats are known for their sleek black coats and distinctive copper eyes.

For Rough-and-Tumble

WINNER Bombay

This breed is playful, demands constant attention and likes to roughhouse with its owners. A cross between a Burmese and a midnight-black American shorthair, the Bombay was created in the 1950s by a breeder determined to produce a house cat resembling a black panther. They earned championship pedigree status in 1976.

▼ RUNNER-UP Sphynx

Ranked as the most affectionate cat breed by the *Journal of Veterinary Behavior*, the Sphynx enjoys being around people and, some experts say, literally gravitates to owners for warmth.

For Getting Along With Dogs

WINNER Abyssinian
The quiet, reserved Abyssinian is the perfect partner in crime for a canine. Known as the Child of the Gods, due to their close resemblance to the sacred cats of the ancient Egyptians, they were once thought to be feline-rabbit hybrids. Now, breeders know that these highly intelligent cats and their soft, textured coats were imported from Ethiopia around 1868.

▼ **RUNNER-UP**
Japanese Bobtail
One of the oldest cat breeds, the athletic Japanese Bobtail passionately loves its human family, but also gets along famously with other household pets.

For Catching Mice

WINNER American Shorthair
Got a rodent problem? This breed is a mouse hunter like no other, due to its intelligence, sharp claws and barn-cat ancestry. Domestic cats have been purring in America since as early as the 1500s, when Europeans began visiting the New World on ships bearing cats to protect their grain from mice. The American Shorthair's origins are undeniably European. In fact, the first registered pedigreed American Shorthair in the U.S. was a British import named Belle.

▼ RUNNER-UP Maine Coon
Strong, fast and originally bred for mousing, Maine coons make ideal defenders of the family home from rodents and pests.

For Workers Gone During the Day

WINNER British Shorthair
Sweet, undemanding, gentle and quiet, the British Shorthair makes the perfect pet for those who spend a lot of time working, either in or out of the home. If you want focus and quiet during work hours, but a loving feline waiting for you once the deadlines are met, then an independent cat capable of looking after itself is the way to go. This Shorthair's ancestors were likely imported to the British Isles by Roman colonists roughly 2,000 years ago.

RUNNER-UP Russian Blue
Quiet, genteel and quite reserved, the Russian Blue can spend hours at home alone without undue anxiety—but expects play and attention when you get home.

The Blue British Shorthair is highly prized, thanks to its distinctive look and plush blue coat.

Ragdolls are extremely affectionate and in tune with their human's emotions.

For People Who Like to Cuddle

WINNER Ragdoll

The Ragdoll is exceptionally calm and loving, with soft, silky fur that doesn't matt—and a penchant for going completely limp when picked up. Ragdolls are placid, yet playful, making them the perfect furballs for a cuddle party. Legend has it that the breed's gentle nature is due to government experiments performed on Josephine, the matriarch of the Ragdoll, after she was injured; interventions gone awry then led to a genetically altered future for her offspring. (This is, of course, nonsense, but gives the ultimate lap cat mystique just the same.)

RUNNER-UP Ragamuffin

Big, docile Ragamuffin cats are cuddly and affectionate.

PART 4

HUMAN-CAT CONNECTION

From body language to meows to pure intuition, here's a guide to penetrating the mind of your cat.

YOU HAD ME AT "MEOW"

How the meow became the universal language for cats vocalizing to their humans.

Sophie, a cat in my building, is a talker. When her human returns home from work, Sophie greets her at the door meowing, as though she has big news about her day. Her sounds often end with exclamation points—there's no mistaking her excitement. Other times, Sophie's meows clearly demand food, urgent and impatient. Frequently, she sounds more like a bird than a cat—she trills and chirps in short melodic bursts. This chatty nature is one of Sophie's most endearing traits. Was she born a talker? Did her owner yammer at her so much when she was a kitten that she trained her to reply? Did human domestication catalyze the language of cats?

Kittens have always tried to get the attention of their mothers through the classic meow.

79

Susanne Schötz, associate professor of phonetics at Sweden's Lund University, specializes in feline vocalizations and human-cat communication. She doesn't believe meowing began with domestication and says it might appear that way because of how often adult cats meow at humans. However, cats do meow at one another when they need or want something. She says newborn kittens learn this method of signaling needs to their mothers and that "adult cats sometimes use meow-like sounds when looking for a partner or a playmate."

TAKING LANGUAGE LESSONS AT HOME

It was domestication that taught cats how to use meows to communicate with humans. The human sense of smell pales next to that of the feline, so we can't recognize each other (or our pets) through chemicals and pheromones. Our eyes are often focused elsewhere. So cats have learned that using sound to get our attention is the best bet.

Domestication also may have changed the quality or timbre of cats' meows. Specifically, the meow "often resembles the cry of a small child: it can be equally loud, of similar pitch [often quite high] and usually has the same strained voice quality," Schötz says.

Humans are biologically programmed to respond immediately to these sounds, so

A cat seeking human attention is likely to mimic the sound of a needy infant.

Cats aren't shy about vocalizing their needs.

mimicking a human child's cry is an incredibly effective attention-getting mechanism. Perhaps not surprisingly, cats leverage human biology to get what they want.

Our felines are also primed to receive communication from us. According to research, a cat can identify its owner's voice, and will have a greater observable response to it than to someone else's voice. But unlike dogs, who tend to walk over to their owners, cats demonstrate responsiveness by turning their heads or perking up their ears. In other words, your cat knows you're talking to him. (And, if he doesn't respond, he's just choosing to ignore you.)

SMALL TALK AND SOCIAL BONDING

I asked Professor Schötz whether humans and cats can ever have back-and-forth conversations—and whether cats like to communicate with their humans when not asking to sate their hunger or fill some other biological need. Do cats engage in the equivalent of small talk with humans when they share their homes?

While Schötz suspects that this happens, she says it is often difficult to record the "conversations" because they take place in private moments, such as when people are getting ready for bed or are getting dressed in the morning. She thinks small-talk meowing "has something to do with social bonding, which strengthens the relationship

A cat responds to touch from a human by purring with affection.

Scratch your cat under the chin, and you are likely to elicit purrs. But these vibrations can indicate hunger or pain, as well.

83

between the cat and the owner," but she can't say for sure. She hopes to conduct research in the future in which she studies such human-feline "chats" to learn more about the linguistic and communicative functions of "cat speak" and the kind of intimate exchange beings engage in when they are truly close.

FINDING PURR-FECTION

Next to the meow, the most famous cat vocalization is the purr. Owners everywhere seek purring as confirmation that their cats enjoy what they're doing. Purring is the perfect feedback loop for a cat—you can scratch Sophie under the chin until she starts purring, and the longer you scratch the more luxurious the purrs become.

But research from 2009 suggests that purring is more complex than an auditory thumbs-up to a special person—cats purr when they interact with one another, too. And just as cats' meows change depending on context and meaning, their purrs do as well. Interestingly, a purring cat asking for food may make a more "urgent" and "less pleasant" sound. Audio analysis revealed higher-frequency meows within these purrs. Scientists aren't sure whether all food-driven cats change their purrs in this way or whether their findings apply only to cat-human interactions. This is another example of cats using their voices to get people to do what they want—according to researchers,

Cats learn to combine sounds and body language to get what they want.

The more you talk to your cat at home, the more vocal and communicative that cat will be.

85

purrs may also exploit human "sensitivity to acoustic cues" associated with caring for babies.

PITCH AND MELODY

One of the most surprising aspects of Schötz's work involves the melody and inflections of feline vocalization. Cat expression, it turns out, includes a wide range of sounds that can vary in pitch (including the melody), in length and in voice quality. Cats even vary vowel and consonant sounds in their vocalizations—"depending on the context, as well as their mental and emotional state."

Just as human voices have different pitches and styles, so, too, do meows. Cats, like humans, also vary the tones of their voices throughout the day for various reasons. Just as our vocal variations indicate how we feel, so do those of cats. For all Schötz and her colleagues have learned about human-cat communication, she acknowledges there's still much to discover.

Research suggests that the vocalizations of domestic cats differ from those of feral cats, which means human company impacts the way cats speak. Schötz tells me that owners play a big role in how much their cats talk. All the time that Sophie has spent with her human over the years has, apparently, helped to shape her chatty personality. I can't wait to hear what she utters next. —*Joelle Renstrom* 🐾

Affection can be felt through sounds and body language

DECIPHERING THE FELINE VOCABULARY

It may not be on Google Translate—yet—but there's scientific work being done to understand just what our cats are really telling us.

If you own a talkative cat like I do, you know not all meows are alike. There's the "hey, what's up?" meow, the "please pet me" meow, the "FEED ME NOW!" meow and many more. Scientific studies confirm that cats have numerous types of vocalizations, and research suggests domestic cats have a larger and more complex vocabulary than wild cats, as well as most other carnivorous mammals. The big question is: What are our cats saying?

Susanne Schötz, a phonetics professor and author of *The Secret Language of Cats: How to Understand Your Cat for a Better, Happier Relationship*, has devoted much of her professional life to answering that question. While she's learned a lot about feline vocalizations, the fundamental fact remains that "cats do not have a language that works like a human language," she says. Even when she thinks she has a handle on what a cat sound means, she can "never be 100 percent sure" about her interpretation, because of

No words needed: This cat is trying to puff its body up to look as large as possible to scare away predators.

the pitfalls of trying to translate a nonhuman language into a human one.

Despite the challenges, researchers such as Schötz have begun compiling something like a feline dictionary. One of the most interesting findings is about purring, which is a notable vocalization because it is both ingressive and egressive—that is, cats purr both when inhaling and exhaling. Aside from snoring, this type of articulation is fairly unusual. Charles Darwin was particularly interested in feline purring for this reason. The meaning of a purr has always seemed straightforward: feline contentedness. But research challenges this hypothesis, as scientists have observed cats purring in numerous other situations, including when hungry, in pain or even in labor. Cat behaviorists believe purring's primary purpose is to demonstrate that a cat isn't a threat. Schötz's analysis identifies variations between the purrs of individual cats, suggesting nuance in the sound and its meaning.

Schötz spearheaded a project called "Meowsic," which focuses on the phonetic characteristics of cat sounds, as well as how humans perceive them. Following are some of the sounds Schötz and her team, as well as other researchers in the field, have identified.

Cats use an organ in their mouths to take in scent.

MEOW
The most common cat sound has many variations and possible meanings. A meow can be demanding, assertive, affectionate, annoyed or discontented. Meows can even be silent.

PURR
Happy ("I like what you're doing"), hungry, stressed, hurting and/or "I'm not dangerous."

SQUEAK
This high-pitched, short sound often indicates a request.

HISSING
A short, breathy sound made with an open mouth and bared teeth that indicates a cat feels startled and/or threatened. Spitting is a more extreme and demonstrative form of hissing.

MATING CALL
During spring nights, cats in heat make a sound like someone dying. The mating cry is aggressive, demanding—and incredibly loud.

TRILL
A high-pitched warbling sound sometimes used with a meow. Cats make this friendly sound when they're playing, or when an amiable human or feline approaches.

CHIRP / CHATTER
Cats make these birdlike sounds when they're imitating prey during a hunt. They chirp, chirrup or chatter when they're spellbound looking out the window at a squirrel or bird.

HOWL
A threatening sound often combined with growling or snarling, as well as teeth-baring.

MIAOW The kind of meow cats use to communicate with their owners to indicate that they want something. The miaow may be the adult form of the mew.

MOAN This lower-pitched, longer sound can suggest sadness or a need.

MEW This high-pitched meow is used by wanting kittens or distressed adults.

BODY LANGUAGE

ALL THE RIGHT MOVES

From eye and ear movements to positions of whiskers
and tail, your cat's body language reveals what's in his heart and mind.

The position
of a cat's tail
suggests
emotions from
friendliness
to fear.

TAIL

Wagging tail
The wagging tail means
the cat is attentive—but
the more the tail
wags, the more upset the
cat might be getting.

Horseshoe-shaped tail
If the tip of the tail
is raised up in the shape
of a horseshoe,
that's really friendly.

Raised tail
If the tail is still but raised,
that's a friendly signal,
especially from a kitten.

EARS

Ears pointed back
If ears are bent back,
the cat is afraid.

Ears pointed forward
This ear position means
the cat is focusing on you.

Do not have a staring contest with a strange cat—he will see it as aggressive and challenging.

The more fearful a cat becomes, the wider her pupils expand.

95

WHISKERS

Whiskers bent back
This means that the
cat is anxious—or at least,
pretty uncomfortable.

Whiskers bent forward
Much like when
ears are bent forward,
this means the
cat is at attention.

Whiskers are
sensitive tactile
hairs that grow
on a cat's muzzle
and elsewhere
on his body.

When on his hind legs, a cat can be playing—or trying to ward off predators.

EYES

Dilated pupils
A cat can dilate his pupils when surprised or stimulated.

Constricted pupils
When pupils are constricted, the cat may feel tense.

Staring
We've all been subject to the feline stare. Be careful—this can be a cat challenging you.

Blinking
When a cat blinks at you, she's likely feeling safe.

THE BODY

Erect body
If the cat puts her whole body erect—the tail is like a large brush and the fur is piled up—she is in a protective stance, trying to make herself look big for self-defense.

Cats don't usually recognize themselves in the mirror, but can easily ID friends with their sense of smell.

YOUR BRILLIANT KITTY

Is your pet an Einstein? The latest research into cat intelligence reveals their social smarts.

Can your cat: Respond to his or her name? Tell the difference between your voice and that of a stranger? Easily locate a toy hidden behind a solid object, say, a piece of furniture? If the answer to all these questions is yes, it's a sign that your kitty is pretty smart, according to feline behaviorist Kristyn Vitale, PhD, a cat researcher at Oregon State University's Human-Animal Interaction Lab.

Today, Felis silvestris catus is one of the world's most popular pets, with an estimated 600 million of them living in households worldwide. "I think the ability of cats to be very flexible in their behavior is one reason they've been so popular," Vitale says. "They can do well in an apartment or on a farm."

Surprisingly, relatively little research to date has been devoted to cat cognition, or their internal mental processes, especially compared with the sizable number of studies conducted on dogs' mental processes.

Vitale is attempting to correct that. She's one of a small number of researchers studying feline cognition, which, she says, differs from intelligence. She says that cognition is "how an individual cat is thinking about something." Intelligence, she says, "is more how they are using what they think about something to act upon it in

"is a cognitive milestone for human infants," says Vitale. Evidence for the skill in felines comes from several studies showing that they can easily solve "visible displacement" tests in which they see an object disappear and search for it where it was last seen. Researchers say that not only do cats easily solve this type of test but that the older they are, the better they become at solving the problems posed.

> # Cats have 250 million cortical neurons, compared to 530 million for dogs and 16 billion for us.

an intelligent way...a way that we perceive as being smart. It's a fine line between the two."

Until now, researchers have focused mainly on cats' physical cognition, for example, hearing, sight and smell. All these senses play an important role for cats from birth, especially smell, since kittens are born blind but with functioning olfactory systems. "Cats' strong sense of smell is definitely a source of their intelligence and a major means by which they perceive the world," according to Vitale.

Another aspect of cat physical cognition that was studied early on is "object permanence"— recognizing that when an object disappears from sight it continues to exist. This kind of recognition

Yet another early study looked at whether cats have an internal clock. It stands to reason they would, Vitale says, because felines are active during dusk and dawn. "Having natural cycles, knowing when they need to hunt and need to rest, makes sense for them."

Notably, when cats live alongside us, they're smart enough to readjust their natural behaviors, she says. "He got out of bed. That's a signal. It's light outside, so it's time to eat. Many of these things get associated and cats track them that way." This is called associative learning.

PICKING UP ON CUES

Vitale's lab focuses on cats' social cognition, or how they perceive

Cats can sharpen cognitive skills with indoor toys that help them simulate the act of hunting.

Many felines have a natural preference for either chasing things on the ground or batting objects in the air.

103

The Siamese is one of the most intelligent and socially deft domestic breeds.

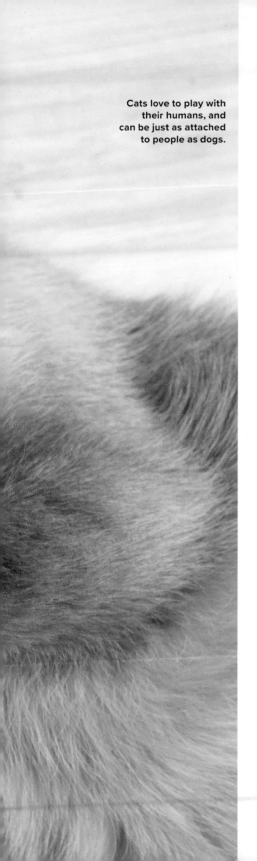

Cats love to play with their humans, and can be just as attached to people as dogs.

Five Ways to Evaluate Your Cat's Intelligence

ALL FOUR OF KRISTYN Vitale's cats (Bo, Macy, Carl and Kevin), know to sit, come and stand. "It's something they do every day," the cat cognition researcher says. "I have all of them sit for their food." But Bo is especially intelligent. "He knows the commands stand, high jump, jump over an obstacle, high-five, ring a service bell and more."

Most people are skeptical when Vitale explains that cats are smart enough to be trained, but they need only watch her YouTube training videos (maueyes.com) to be convinced. Signs of intelligence: If your cat quickly learns new tricks; can easily differentiate between different events and/or items; rapidly solves food puzzles; or is very responsive to your emotions, gestures or pointing cues. Consider these five ways to determine if your cat is a kitty Einstein.

1 Show your cat a favorite toy (like a catnip-filled "mouse"). Place the toy behind a piece of furniture where it is relatively easily accessible. Watch his behavior. Does he (a) immediately retrieve the toy; (b) stay put?

2 Hide a treat or toy and see how long it takes kitty to find it: Put one treat under a cup to your left and another one under a cup to your right. Point to the cup you want the cat to go to. Only give the treat if she goes to the correct cup. Do this 10 times. **How often does she choose because you point at it,** rather than because she smells it: (a) 7 out of 10 approaches; (b) fewer than 7 approaches.

3 Put a treat or toy inside an egg carton and see if your cat can open the carton. **Does he do this:** (a) very fast; (b) very slow.

4 See if your cat can understand your behavior. Sit on the floor. Ignore your cat for one minute, then pay attention to him for one minute. **Does his behavior change, depending on your attention toward him? In other words, does** he: (a) interact with you in some way; (b) ignore you completely.

5 Can your cat differentiate between two shapes? Cut out a large circle and a square from a thick piece of paper. Place the shapes in front of your cat. At first, reward him or her for tapping either shape. This gets them used to touching the shapes. Choose which shape you want to train your cat to recognize. If it's the circle, only give a treat for touching the circle. **Does your cat** (a) catch on quickly and tap only the circle; (b) rarely get it right.

If your cat got mostly "a's"— congratulations—she is a quick learner! If your cat got mostly "b's," try providing additional stimulation to nurture intelligence. This can include enrichment training, interactive toys, cat furniture for climbing and food puzzles, as well as exposure to novel stimuli.

and act upon social stimuli in their environment. One way to test for social cognition is to examine how cats pick up on human cues. This is called social referencing, or a cat's ability to use a person's emotional reactions to evaluate an unfamiliar situation and adjust his or her behavior as needed.

In one test, Vitale has a cat owner act either afraid or happy toward an object, in this case, a fan with streamers, which a cat might well find frightening. Vitale waits to see if the cat picks up its human's emotional cues. "If the owner's afraid," Vitale asks, "is the cat behind the owner, looking nervously at the item? If the owner's happy, is the cat next to him or her, trying to interact and looking at the item?" Socially smart cats will pick up on their owners' emotional states.

ABILITY TO BOND

Another measure of social cognition Vitale has been researching is the attachment bond. Cats and their humans are brought into the lab together. "Then we take the owner out, leaving the cat alone in the room. We bring the owner back in two minutes later and there's a reunion." When reunited with their human, some cats greet their person, "then go back to exploring the room." These cats are securely attached, according to Vitale. Other cats go to their human and cling to them. That, says Vitale,

is an insecure response. "They're still upset that the owner left." She adds, "We also have cats that don't really respond when their owner returns; they sit at a distance and ignore the owner," a sign that bonding is incomplete.

These attachment styles might correspond to the cat's earliest weeks and months of life. Studies on how early sensory experiences influence brain development and perception found that cats between 3 and 9 weeks of age need to spend time around, and interact with, people to develop healthy socialization behaviors with us. In other words, early interaction with people generally makes for friendlier cats.

Early training can help cats stay attuned to human cues like finger-pointing. Indeed, a study from cognitive ethologist Ádám Miklósi, PhD, DSc, and colleagues found that, in general, cats can find food when a human points to it. A later study suggests that cats can even distinguish between people's voices, and that our vocalizations elicit measurable changes in behavior.

People view cats as independent, aloof and self-centered, Vitale says. But when they see how social some of these animals are in her videos, the arguments stop. "With millions of cats in our homes," she concludes, "it's really important to understand their behavior and how they process the world." 🐾

Regular stimulation helps keep cats mentally sharp.

Cats rely on sounds and movements to tell you just how they really feel.

Your cat is watching you and might get upset when you leave, so be sure to say goodbye.

HOW TO READ YOUR CAT

Seeing the world through your pet's eyes
requires an intuitive mentality.

When a friend told me about a successful experience with an animal communicator, I had to try it. Zola, my companion since college, is 21, and while I know she has chronic kidney disease and must be feeling the effects of old age, we can't exactly discuss her symptoms over breakfast. Despite how well I know her, I worry that she's in pain or that I may not recognize when she's past the point of enjoying life. Curiosity was also a motivating factor—why not give animal communicators a try?

Animal communicators attempt to glean information about pets' health, happiness and overall well-being by using their own specifically honed intuitions. The animal communicator I used, Dawn Allen, has practiced for over 20 years. She studied holistic methods of working with animals at Goddard College and got certified in TTouch, a dog-training protocol that consists of body and behavioral work. After she learned about animal communication, she decided to make it her focus.

Animal communicator Jennifer Dickman entered the vocation after a lifetime of experiences in which she's encountered extraordinary connections to animals—everything from a herd of sheep to parakeets. Dickman's first experience involved communicating with an instructor's cat, and Dickman's perceptions from the cat were so spot-on that her instructor urged her to pursue this type of interspecies communication as a career. Dickman says it's hard to describe how she communicates with animals, but intuition lies at the heart of the practice. Upon spending time with an animal, Dickman receives "impressions," which can be physical or emotional, and often take the form of images and feelings. Those impressions allow communicators to ask pet owners questions about everything from daily routines to food types to specific behavior.

During my session with Allen, after a few minutes of silence she said, "What a delight Zola is! And wow, does she ever love you." This was a good start—Zola is delightful and she does love me to pieces. From there, Allen got more specific, noting that Zola is often full of manic energy, and that despite being old she's prone to hyperactivity. She went on to say

> Telepathy is an impossible superpower, but using intuition to understand your cat is a skill.

> Even a cat who is medically well cared for can benefit from insight into her inner life, sensations and sense of personal space.

Your cat may find it hard
to communicate his
needs and emotions,
or his aches and pains.

that this often manifests at night via yowling and agitation. Part of the reason for my call was Zola's caterwauling at night in such a distressed fashion that I wasn't sure if she was in pain or had forgotten where I was (or where she was). Allen told me Zola has little short-term memory left, which means she might forget whether I'm in the house or not, even if she was on my lap 30 seconds earlier. When Zola prowls around the house yowling, especially at night, she may be looking for me.

Stories from others abound. Isaac Sparks, a cat owner from Portland, Maine, called Allen after his cat Stella had begun using the bathroom on his and his girlfriend's shoes and backpack. During their session, Allen suggested that Stella didn't like it when they left. Thus, the cat had been marking objects associated with them leaving the apartment: shoes and backpacks. But since it's impossible to stay at home all the time, Allen advised the couple to "say goodbye before leaving the apartment and to let her know they'd be back." The couple began doing just that, and according to Sparks, Stella "never peed on another backpack or pair of shoes."

You might question why I contacted a communicator instead of a vet. Well, I was already treating Zola medically, and still needed another path to connect. Literal mind-reading—knowing another's thoughts and feelings through psychic telepathy—is likely an impossible feat. Telepathy would be a superpower, but intuition is a skill. And sometimes, a little insight into the minds of our feline familiars is just what pet owners crave.

—*Joelle Renstrom*

SIX WAYS TO STAY ATTUNED TO YOUR CAT'S INNER LIFE

1 Know Thyself
Cats respond to human emotions and take emotional cues from their owners. Just as feelings of stress or anxiety can be "contagious" among humans, they can transfer to cats as well. If you notice your cat is behaving strangely, reflect on your own emotions and behavior—if you're acting differently, that may be the reason your cat is, too.

2 Get in Tune With His Basic Needs
Cats have basic needs that, if unmet, will throw them into turmoil. In this way, a cat is very much like a child—if a child is unhappy, there are obvious explanations: she is hungry; he needs to be changed; she's in physical discomfort; he wants attention. Those possibilities apply to cats, too. Does the cat have enough food and water? Is her litter clean? Is his fur clean and untangled? Does she have good hiding spots or a good perch to watch the action? When was the last time you played with your fluffy friend? Is your cat getting exercise—and does he have plenty of toys? Cats often get into trouble when they're bored. Cats like their space, too, and boxes are big hits with (and safe spaces for) most felines.

3 Remember Your Cat's Roots
According to Thomas McNamee, author of *The Inner Lives of Cats*, domestic cats aren't so evolutionarily distant from North African wildcats. "A lot of your cat's weird behavior is the same as the wildcat's, and once you understand it as such—the rubbing, the sniffing, the need for a high observation post, her obsession with her litter box—maybe you'll cut her some slack," he writes. You may find that indulging some of these tendencies makes your cat happier.

4 Use Your Powers of Observation
Cats are generally less communicative than dogs, which means we need to pay more attention to their behaviors. Daily routines give owners the ability to observe and learn. When is your cat hungriest? Does your cat eat more or less when you're gone at work during the day? Does the cat seem to prefer salmon to turkey, or liver pâté to beef? What do you

Is this alert cat quizzical, or does she feel sick?

notice when you clean the litter box? The analogy to children again applies here—one of the grossest parts of parenthood is becoming intimately familiar with your kid's bodily functions. You know every time a child spits up or goes to the bathroom, and you know the composition of the stuff (even if you'd really rather not). You know if it's been four days since the last time your kid went No. 2. Having the same information about your cat provides a lot of insight and allows an owner to make some beneficial adjustments, like administering kitty laxatives.

5 It's in the Eyes

Cats have staring contests with one another as a means of establishing dominance—the first one to blink loses. Cats will blink, quickly look away, and/or narrow their eyes to indicate that they're not inviting such a staring contest and don't present a threat. Thus, shy, newly adopted or feral cats may avert their gaze from human eyes to play it safe. Comfortable cats usually will make direct eye contact with their owners. One way to tell if a cat is relaxed is whether her pupils are normal-sized; pupil dilation

suggests heightened anxiety. Long, slow blinks (as distinct from the typical blink that moistens the eyes) demonstrate relaxation and affection. And when a cat closes his eyes in your presence, that means he trusts you.

6 It's the Cat, Not You

Cats are harder to read than dogs, which is why they're often referred to as "aloof," "independent" or "mysterious." Fear that cats spread the plague were prompted by Pope Gregory IX when he declared cats evil and servants of Satan in the 1200s. According to David Grimm, author of *Citizen Canine: Our Evolving Relationship With Cats and Dogs*, whereas humans actively began selecting for dogs skilled at hunting or serving as companions immediately upon their integration into human society, we left cats to their own devices and tolerated them only because they killed mice. "So dog domestication happened for tens of thousands of years, but cat domestication just stopped," says Grimm. If you're having trouble getting attuned to your cat, remember that evolution has made this an uphill task. Luckily, it's a worthwhile one. 🐾

> ## Cats may not be as communicative as dogs, but they're just as eager to share their feelings and their needs with you.

Cats can get bored just hanging out all day—they need entertainment options, too.

IN TRAINING

YOUR CAT CAN DO WHAT?

Long after your cat has been socialized, you can teach him to shake hands, walk with a leash and give a high five.

Training helps to create a strong bond of communication between you and your cat.

117

They say you can't teach an old dog new tricks. But surprisingly, you can teach cats of any age to sit, shake hands and even wake you up.

Training "helps to create a stronger bond of communication between you and your pet," says Shawn Simons, headmistress of Kitty Bungalow: Charm School for Wayward Cats in Los Angeles, the only 100 percent street-cat rescue and feral-cat socialization facility in California. To place any cat in a home, socializing is key. "In order to be successful in training, you and your cat have to listen and to respond to each other. Training can help your cat overcome social fears and live a more robust life," Simons explains. From feral to domesticated cats, training can help shy cats become less anxious and more social—and create a peaceable environment for everyone.

"Cats [like dogs] need to start learning how to interact with people when they are very young," between 2 and 8 weeks of age, say animal behavior specialists John Bradshaw and Sarah Ellis in their book, *The Trainable Cat*. Bradshaw and Ellis offer a crucial insight when it comes to helping cats learn: Our felines will "flee any situation they find aversive," so if they associate unpleasant feelings with you, their affection "will instantly diminish. Even mild punishments that cause only minor discomfort and merely startle the cat will have this effect."

Instead, to train your cat, you must understand how cats learn. First, set the scene. Offer a home with enticements like delicious food, clean water, heating pads, dry beds, toys, medicine and cuddles. "Dogs are easier to train, not because they are smarter but because they have more avenues of reward," Simons says. "Exercise, petting and treats are all ways to reward a dog. For a cat—it is just about the treats. Now, this makes things difficult if your cat seems unmotivated by the treats at hand. But that doesn't mean you can't train them; it means you have some shopping to do to find out what treat actually motivates them. Recently, we started using Churu

> Cats that master tricks—like paw-shaking, sitting, even using the toilet—are much likelier to be adopted out of a shelter to a human home—and to stay put.

A target stick, like a conductor's wand, can boost focus and direct the action.

Keep training sessions short—cats can quickly get bored.

Clicker training can help to enhance the bond between a pet cat and a human owner.

Cats learn to link the sound of a clicker to a coming treat or other reward.

treats at the Bungalow for training. [The cats] love them!"

Bradshaw and Ellis, meanwhile, note that just as with humans, the best learning comes when cats are free of distraction. Conduct training in a quiet place that your cat finds familiar. And beware that cat distractions may be different than yours: "Cats, with their acute senses of smell and hearing, can be distracted by things we barely notice"—from the faint odor of meat or chicken defrosting in another room to birds outside a window. Before training your cat, make sure that water and a litter box are available, for maximum comfort. And, say the experts, don't train your cat on a full stomach. A healthy desire for that special reward is key.

Once your cat has been trained to socialize, he can learn a few tricks at any age. "At our rescue, the most popular tricks are leash training and high fives," says Simons, who finds that rescue cats capable of a few fun moves—signs of friendliness—are easier to place. "People find it hard to walk away from a cat that just gave them five, up high!" ❖

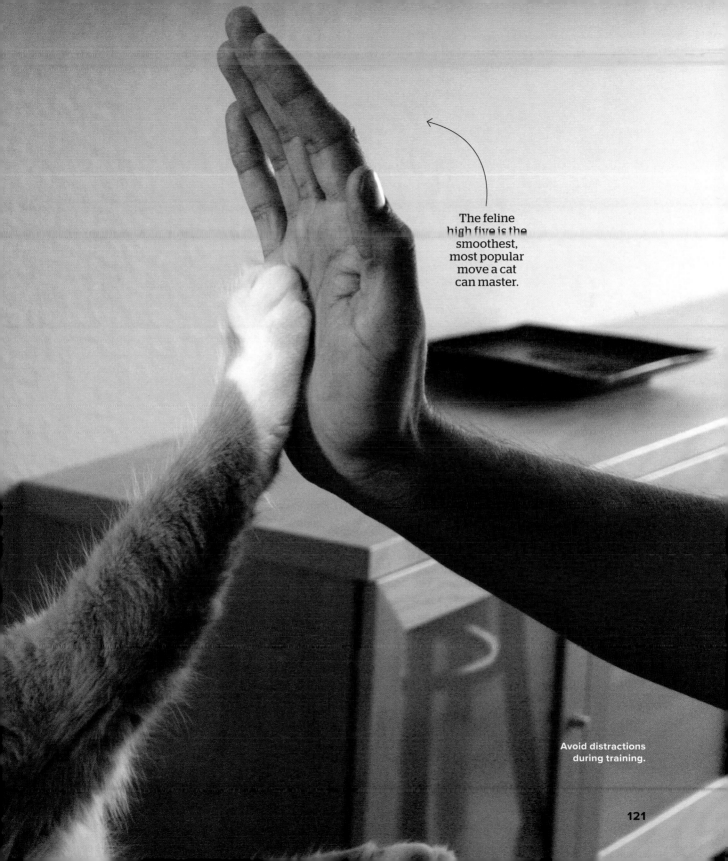

The feline
high five is the
smoothest,
most popular
move a cat
can master.

Avoid distractions
during training.

GETTING AN EDUCATION

CAT TRAINING 101
FOUR RULES FOR THE ROAD

People don't traditionally train cats, because they think of cats as... independent and full of free will," says Sarah Ellis, co-author of *The Trainable Cat*. However, cats can learn to scratch a post instead of the couch, get into the cat carrier without a fight, and master tricks such as rolling over and shaking hands (paws). Cats can even be trained to use the toilet!

To train your cat, follow these four guidelines, and you won't go wrong.

1 Use Positive Reinforcement
Rewarding good behavior with treats (or attention, if your cat isn't food-motivated) incentivizes that behavior—and why wouldn't your pet want rewards?

2 Start Early
If you want to keep your new cat from jumping up onto the table or scratching your brand new rug, redirecting the behavior with positive reinforcement will be more successful the earlier you start. Then you don't have to break the cat's bad habits but rather just establish some new, positive ones.

3 Call a Consultant
For really tricky cat conundrums, behavioral experts offer their services via home visits, phone calls or Skype/FaceTime. Cat consultant Mikel Delgado's organization, Feline Minds, offers consultations, homework assignments and follow-up support. You can also ask your vet for recommendations or search online, but be sure that whichever expert you choose is certified. Websites for the International Association of Animal Behavior Consultants, Certified Applied Animal Behaviorists and the American College of Veterinary Behaviorists have searchable directories of certified consultants.

4 Try Clickers
Clickers make a sound when you press a button (there are also clicker apps). The purpose of a clicker is to link the sound and the reward. Once the cat makes that association, the clicker becomes the signal for the cat to do what you've asked so it gets a treat. Scientists concur: According to a study published in the October 2017 issue of *Animals*, the training has the potential "to modify unwanted behaviors and enhance the human-animal bond." 🐾

With practice (and treats) your cat will learn to respond.

AT-HOME CAT TRAINING

TRICKS YOU CAN TEACH YOUR CAT WITH A CLICKER

Cat trainer Shawn Simons of Kitty Bungalow uses a handheld clicker along with food rewards to teach her shelter cats the showier, more complex tricks that aid in their adoption. Simons offers some advice and tips on teaching your own cat a few new tricks.

YOU WILL NEED

A CLICKER You can find them at pet stores, and Simons suggests getting one with a wrist strap.

TREATS Get special snacks used only for training—look for them at your pet store or vet's office.

TARGET STICK Find these in pet stores, or use a pencil or chopstick with a ping-pong ball at the end.

HELPFUL HINTS

- Train before meals so your cat is hungry and motivated by the treats.
- Train in a room with few distractions.
- Don't burn your cat out in the training sessions. Keep them short (five minutes) and rely on repetition over time.
- Create an association between the sound of the clicker and the treats.
- Have the clicker in one hand along with treats. Hold the target stick in your other hand. Repeat.

SIT

Move the target stick above your cat's head. Her curiosity will get her to point her nose toward the target and move her rump toward the ground (be patient). When her rump reaches the ground, click and give her a treat. Do this four or five times, give her a rest and then try again later. Once she gets the idea, you can begin incorporating the word "sit" into the training. While holding the target stick above her head, say "Sit" as soon as she sits. Click, then offer a treat. Soon she will associate the command "Sit" with the action of sitting. Eventually, your cat will be able to perform without a stick or treats.

Training tools
can ease
the learning
process.

PAW SHAKE

Dogs don't have the market on this easy-to-teach trick. Lift one of your cat's front paws. With your other hand, use your clicker and give him a treat. Repeat four to five minutes, then give him a rest. If your cat lifts his paw during the training, immediately click and give him the treat. Eventually incorporate the word "shake" into the training.

HIGH FIVE

Show her the treat first and then put it between your middle and ring finger, palm up in a high-five. She may sniff the treat or try to grab it with her mouth. Wait until she tries to reach for it with her paw. When she touches your hand, click and give her the treat. Repeat this four or five times, until she understands the concept. Eventually incorporate a training command of "high five."

WALK ON LEASH

"Training doesn't always mean learning to do showy tricks," says Simons. Leash training can help reduce stress when visiting the vet and allow your cat to experience the outdoors in safety. "Be prepared for your walks to meander more than your average 5k." The start of leash training doesn't involve a leash at all. It simply involves the harness. Just before dinner, put the harness on your cat when he is standing near his bowl. Make sure you have upgraded dinner to his favorite food, making the harness part of a special treat. "Dress" your cat for dinner every night. Once he gets into his "dinner clothes" without complaint, start dressing him in another room. Allow him to walk in the harness to the food bowl. When he is comfortable wearing the harness, snap on the leash—but do not pull or lead him. Just let it drag and remove it along with the harness. After he is very comfortable dragging the leash, take him into your backyard to explore the world together.

CARRIER TRAINING

Getting your cat into the carrier is a common problem for cat owners. But training your cat to enter the carrier without complaint could make a big difference in an emergency situation. Get a cute carrier so you don't mind leaving it out. Put your cat's favorite toy in the carrier and allow her to inspect the outside and inside of the carrier on her own. Once she is comfortable, lift her gently and place her in the carrier for only a few minutes. Give her a special treat and release her. Repeat until she associates the carrier with the special treat. Gradually extend the time inside. Now begin putting the carrier into your car during these sessions, always increasing time and releasing with a treat. Then it's time to ride! Take her somewhere other than the vet—perhaps the pet store, where she can pick out a new toy. She won't associate the carrier with the veterinarian, and she'll have pleasant memories of treats and toys. 🐾

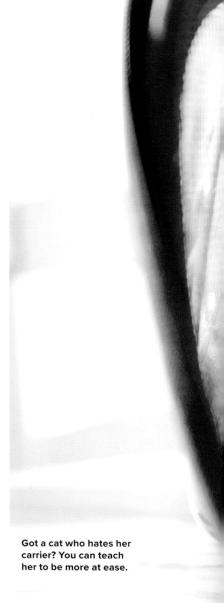

Got a cat who hates her carrier? You can teach her to be more at ease.

PART 5

HELPING YOUR CAT THRIVE

Feeding, playing, health care, companionship:
how to nurture, entertain and care for the feline at home.

NURTURING

BRINGING UP BABY

Raising a kitten to be a great cat.

I have had my cat, Zola, for 21 years, since I was a junior in college. She waits at the top of the stairs when she hears my keys in the door. She comes when I call her, sleeps snuggled against my stomach and has a knack for making me laugh. She's not aloof or indifferent—even dog people like her.

I've always wondered if her upbringing during my wilder years shaped her irresistibly quirky personality. For cats, like kids, both nurture and nature powerfully influence who they become. While no one has absolute control over how their pet (or child) will turn out, owners mold their cats' behaviors and personalities, for better or worse.

First of all, it's important to recognize that personality and behavior aren't the same thing. One might be antisocial but still act chatty and outgoing at a work function. A person has to learn to behave appropriately in various situations, just as pets do—both kids and pets are potty-trained, for example. Behavior can be taught, but personality is comprised of genes, early influences, traumas and other factors, some of which we've not yet identified.

The prime time to socialize kittens is between 2 and 9 weeks of age, according to Mikel Delgado, certified cat behavior consultant and founder of Feline Minds, an organization that offers cat consulting. This is when kittens' brains absorb information like sponges: "They rapidly learn what's safe and dangerous, and it's a good time for them to have good experiences with different people and animals," she notes. Kittens can learn that people are safe, affectionate and fun, which helps them become more social. Acclimating them to the carrier or the car during this period makes vet visits easier on everyone.

The problem, though, is that most of us don't yet have our cats when they're between 2 and 9 weeks old; the average kitten adoption age is around 12 weeks of age. We can't control what or who influenced them before we got them, but we can still affect their temperament over time, primarily by changing their behavior—which owners can do at any point by following some general guidelines.

POSITIVE REINFORCEMENT

Delgado's biggest tip is to "give them experiences that will make them happier," which in turn makes them display more desirable behavior. All cat owners should provide a secure environment, including high spaces from which cats can observe their surroundings; hiding spots; and objects that are appropriate for scratching and playing. Cats need to have some control over their environment, particularly when it comes to ways

Kittens as young as 2 weeks old rapidly learn socialization and behavioral skills.

In kittens, nature and nurture combine to create temperament.

131

A kitten's brain is like a sponge. Teach yours to recognize danger and to have fun.

This kitten is riveted by the camera; those same powers of observation will help her throughout life.

to escape danger or stressful situations, such as loud noises, other animals and toddlers.

Despite their aloof reputation, cats like to hang out with their people. One common complaint among cat owners is the state of their couches. Delgado says the problem is often that cats want to scratch something in the room where everyone else is. So if the scratching post sits in a seldom-used basement room, the cat won't use it; but if you move it into the living room, the cat will. "The best way to change a cat's behavior is to change its humans'

behavior," Delgado says.

Positive reinforcement is the best way to get cats to learn specific behaviors. The downside is how often people inadvertently reward cats for bad behavior. If your cat yowls at night for food and you feed her to quiet her down, you're

teaching her that her behavior yields the reward she desires—and she'll never stop. Getting out of bed or giving her attention also reinforces the behavior. When cats act undesirably, the best course of action is to ignore them—which, of course, is the hardest thing to do.

Keeping a box around is an easy way to get your cat to take the equivalent of a deep breath.

Like humans, cats have a fight-or-flight stress response.

Curling up inside a cardboard box allows cats to generate and maintain heat.

133

Your kitten needs your attention and company.

THE POWER OF ACCEPTANCE

No amount of training or positive reinforcement will guarantee that a cat will be "everything you want them to be," Delgado says. She urges people to accept what their cats want—if your cat doesn't like being held, for example, don't force it.

She also encourages people to have realistic expectations. Cats are not dogs—that doesn't mean they're a lesser animal or companion, but it does necessitate different expectations. Humans domesticated dogs long before we domesticated cats, and dogs were actually bred to be social, to be "man's best friend." Cats were bred to be cats—and maybe to catch some mice. It's only relatively recently, Delgado points out, that we have asked cats to stay indoors and to meet more of our emotional needs.

Still, the idea that cats aren't capable of the same emotional relationships with people is a misconception Delgado wants to debunk. When I tell her that Zola acts "like a dog," I play into one of her pet peeves. "It's not unusual for cats to be very bonded to their owners and crave attention and company," she says. "Your cat is exhibiting cat behavior, not dog behavior." Maybe Zola isn't as exceptional as I think—but ultimately, whether due to nature, nurture, luck or some combination thereof, I don't really care how she got to be the ideal companion.
— *Joelle Renstrom* ❧

A kitten needs mental stimulation and exercise to become a great cat.

Most of a kitten's brain development happens outside of the womb.

135

LEND A HAND

FOSTERING KITTENS

A few short weeks can have a lasting impact on a cat's life.

One way to have an impact on kittens during their most formative time—between 2 and 9 weeks old—is to foster cat moms and offspring during that critical period, alone. It's common that people end up adopting at least one of their foster cats, but even if you don't take one, you can make them more "adoptable and adaptable for others," says cat consultant Mikel Delgado. If more people fostered kittens and—in addition to providing the necessary food, shelter and veterinary care—taught them that people are safe, as well as how to play and interact with both people and animals, then cats might not have the reputation for being so aloof.

Sarah Chauncey, a cat rescue volunteer and manager of the Facebook page P.S. I Love You More Than Tuna, says fostering can also help owners heal from the death of a beloved cat by providing "feline contact without the heartbreak." Not only are people at cat-rescue shelters understanding with and supportive of grieving owners, but volunteering itself helps "break the cycle of rumination that's so common when we're grieving," she says. Given just how goofy, adorable and joyful kittens are, it's easy for anyone to be fully present around them: "They're great teachers of living in the moment," Chauncey adds. 🐾

A newborn kitten is so tiny, she can fit in the palm of your hand.

Kittens start to take their first shaky steps when they are about 3 weeks old and soon become more confident about exploring.

TO PUNISH OR NOT TO PUNISH?

The rationale for putting down the squirt gun.

y friends' cat jumps on the dinner table every time we sit down to eat. Its hair gets in the food; it bats the salt shaker onto the floor and generally is a nuisance. Eventually, they shut the cat in the bedroom, but I always wonder why they don't discourage the behavior with a squirt gun.

"Do you have a squirt gun?" Mikel Delgado asked me when I told her about this scenario.

"Of course," I said. "I kept one on my nightstand when Zola kept me from sleeping."

"I'd advise you to throw away your squirt guns," Delgado said.

What?! The system worked brilliantly. Zola would start her 3 a.m. shenanigans, which usually consisted of her sharpening her claws on the underside of my mattress—and I'd grab the squirt gun, aim under the bed and let her have it. She'd sprint out the door,

and I'd go back to sleep. She didn't keep it up for long and eventually ran away every time I even reached for the squirt gun.

Just as children need discipline, I always assumed that cats do too. But Delgado argues that punishment for cats is inappropriate, because they can't understand what they've done wrong. Making a loud noise scares a cat, and the cat doesn't interpret the noise as a punishment for prior behavior. A cat who gets chased or tossed out of a room might think its owner is playing a game. A squirt gun doesn't deter bad behavior in the long run, says Delgado. "[The cat will] be back on the counter in 10 minutes."

It's crucial to recognize the motivation behind a cat's behavior. Does it crave attention? Does it need to scratch or hide? Is it bored? One common misconception is that cats act out of spite. Say a cat uses your boyfriend's suitcase as a bathroom the day after he moves in. It's easy

to assume the cat doesn't like your boyfriend or it's jealous or angry, but the actual motivation is likely to be more like an unmet need—maybe the cat didn't get much attention during the move, or perhaps the suitcase and other belongings block a favorite hiding spot.

Most behavioral problems can be alleviated by meeting the cat's needs. Is it getting enough exercise? What about mental stimulation? Delgado recommends what she calls "punishments from God" or environmental punishments. If you need to stop a cat from counter-surfing, put a sticky place mat or tape on the counter that makes the experience unenjoyable. If your cat chews on plants or cords, spray them with bitter apple. Wrap tinfoil around the couch leg your cat won't stop scratching. Such environmental deterrents train the cat that these behaviors aren't worth it, without them being directly related to you. —*Joelle Renstrom* ❧

Kittens get into all kinds of trouble. To help them behave, dispense treats, not punishment.

139

INTERSPECIES

CAN CATS AND DOGS GET ALONG?

And can a feline who's been your only fur kid accept a new kitty?

You've heard the cliché about "fighting like cats and dogs" along with the warning that, if given half a chance, a dog would chase and even kill a cat. Yet countless pet owners disagree, reporting their cats and dogs are best buddies at home. The reality is more complex: Our two favorite species can have a lovefest, but are not always happy to be around each other. And introducing animals to each other can lead to serious, potentially dangerous problems—especially for your cat.

The truth is that you will never know what to expect when you bring another fur kid into your home. But you can boost the likelihood of success by planning for a safe initial meet-and-greet between the animals and arranging your home so that each species thrives.

SCIENCE INVESTIGATES THE CAT-DOG COWMBO

Tel Aviv University researchers report that cats and dogs do indeed have the ability to tolerate—and even care for each other. But those skills are enhanced when the two mammals start living together before becoming adults.

The idea that felines and canines are natural-born enemies is a myth.

Living in translation: Dogs and cats that are friends learn each other's body language.

141

Cats and dogs can misread each other: Cats lash their tails when mad, while dogs arch their backs.

Gender (at least if the animals are neutered when old enough) doesn't seem to matter in feline and canine friendship. But socializing dogs before a year of age, and cats prior to 6 months, is helpful in forming the dog-cat bond. Tiny kittens are defenseless and shouldn't be placed around any dog, certainly not a larger rambunctious puppy.

"Young cats have play behavior that dogs pick up on if they grow up with cats. It's amazing to see how they will play and interact with each other," says feline-canine specialist Peter Muller III, DVM, a veterinarian at VCA Briarcliff Animal Hospital, who points to videos his daughter shares of her puppy and kitty growing up together, playing and snoozing side by side.

Of course, introducing a full-grown dog to your cat, or vice versa, can turn out fine, too, especially if the dog does not have a history of aggression with felines. But how do you know if the dog has harmed cats before, if you are adopting from either a shelter or rescue group?

"When dogs are waiting for adoption at a shelter, a common question is 'What is the dog like with cats?'" notes Christy Hoffman, PhD, assistant professor of animal behavior, ecology and conservation at Canisius College in Buffalo, New York.

She explains that shelters use standardized assessments to try and predict dogs' behavior around humans and other dogs—but there isn't a standard, verified way to predict how a dog in a shelter will behave around cats.

Hoffman and her research team tried to find out, using a realistic-looking cat doll, recordings of cat sounds, and the smell of cat urine to see how shelter dogs responded to felines. Some dogs with a history of attacking cats reacted strongly to the cat sounds, but there wasn't a clear reaction to the other stimuli. The findings suggest that one day sound may provide some clues about an individual dog's behavior around cats but, for now, you are on your own.

Even if a shelter has no reason to think a dog is aggressive toward cats, use common sense when introducing a dog to your cat.

PREVENTING THE PROVERBIAL DOG-CAT CHASE SCENE

You may have adopted the friendliest, most gentle dog in the world, but if your cat is greeted by a happy, galloping dog who wants to play, she will likely flee. And so the cycle begins: When cats run, dogs chase. It is a trigger. It does not necessarily mean the dog wants to hurt the cat, but it can get the initial meeting and the relationship off to a rocky start.

"A cat being chased may think it is going to die, even if it's a goofy Labrador just trying to play," says Steve Dale, certified animal

> **Teach your new puppy to chase after balls and other moving objects, not the fragile kitten that shares his home.**

behavior consultant and host of two nationally syndicated radio shows, *Steve Dale's Pet World* and *The Pet Minute*. That's why you need to take precautions when you introduce a dog into your household—or, for that matter, if you bring a cat into a dog-only home.

First, Dale emphasizes, have the dog on a leash and make sure the cat can escape to a high perch or window ledge, into a cat tunnel (sold at pet-supply stores) or even jump into a large, deep box. A gate in a doorway the cat can jump over or walk through—but the dog can't—is also helpful.

"A cat needs an escape route, usually a place the dog will understand it can't go," Dale says.

What is it exactly about cats that sometimes "triggers" dogs to chase them repeatedly or to play too rough or even attack?

"It is not about the cat, it is about the dog," explains veterinary behaviorist Leticia Dantas, DVM, PhD, clinical assistant professor in the University of Georgia Department of Veterinary Biosciences. In some instances, "the dog's socialization history to cats plays a role." Thanks to past experience, the dog may identify cats as prey.

The bottom line: Be very careful when you bring a new dog into your cat's home. Does the dog identify cats as prey or as a potential friend? "Make a realistic choice when selecting a dog," says Dantas. Consult with experts who can guide you in your selection, and have a plan in place to make sure things go well.

EVERY BLENDED FAMILY SHOULD PUT THE CAT IN CHARGE

When a dog and cat meet for the first time, the dog may be perfectly happy and calm and just want to rub, smell or get closer to check out the kitty. Your cat may have already been socialized to dogs and won't feel the need to flee. But as you cautiously let the dog get closer, the feline may have a quick surprise for the canine, showing the dog that the cat is clearly the boss.

"Dogs and cats are so adaptable, and they usually get along fine for the most part. But they are different species and the big difference is that cats have a social order. With more than one cat in a household,

they work out who is the dominant cat. But as far as cats are concerned, dogs don't even fit into the social order," cat health expert Drew Weigner, DVM, president of the Wynn Feline Foundation, says with a laugh.

"Seriously, a cat's attitude when meeting a dog is often like, 'Oh, it's a dog, big deal.' You bring in a dog, it runs up to a cat, the cat scratches the dog on the nose and the dog runs off. Dogs figure out pretty quickly they don't want to get hurt and cats are fully armed. So they won't get in a cat's face, although some playful young dogs and puppies will keep trying for a while."

Even if your new dog-and-cat duo seem simpatico from the get-go, Weigner says it's still a good idea to initially separate the animals until things settle down.

"Then, after a day or two, let the dog into the cat's space and let the cat out to where the dog is. Do that for a few hours at first and let them investigate their smells and you'll likely discover they are accepting each other," he advises. "Once they find each other, it's usually a quick thing like 'Oh, there's a dog, there's a cat. No big deal.'"

Weigner explains, "What you don't want to do is hold the cat in your arms and bring it to the dog. The cat could freak out and you could be injured. It's not a good idea to force the issue. Let them discover each other. It's a little different with kittens.

More supervision might be needed because a small kitten can't defend itself."

A POTENTIALLY BIGGER PROBLEM: INTRODUCING CATS TO EACH OTHER

Weigner, a board-certified feline specialist, established The Cat Doctor, the first cat specialty veterinary practice in the Southeastern U.S., over 30 years ago. "You can imagine how many clients I have seen with cats over the years and many of them have dogs, too. Yet I hardly ever get calls about how to introduce dogs and cats or help them get along. But when they bring another cat into the family, it's a whole different story," he says.

"The thing I hear most is, 'We got another cat and they hate each other! I'm going to have to give it away!' And I explain that, no, they don't.

"The problem is that when you bring a cat into another cat's territory, they are on alert. They know they have to establish a social order—one of the cats has to be dominant," Weigner explains. "It doesn't matter who the top cat will be, and you can't predict it. The cats have to work it out and, until they do, there will be no peace in the kingdom."

What people fear is that the cats will fight and hurt each other. "I tell my clients the fighting has nothing to do with whether the cats like each other; it has to do with who will be the dominant cat. And for the most part, they are

Cats need their own space to hang out and relax.

Importance of a Dog-free Zone

IT MAY BE AN INSTANT LOVEFEST when cat meets dog, but what if your kitty needs a private space to escape a too-playful puppy or ruffled dog? Good news: It's not hard to make a dog-free zone for your cat.

The easiest solution is to put up a child gate (or dog gate) in a doorway. "Wooden ones work best, especially if the cat can walk through it or jump over it and come and go, but the dog can't," explains veterinarian Drew Weigner.

It's important to consider what's in the dog-free zone, too. You'll need to provide water, food and, if windows are placed too high for your cat to look outside, a perch or tall cat tree so your kitty can have a view.

Given some time, most dogs and cats will eventually work out their problems, but even if your pets are friendly, the cat-only space can be a boon.

Dogs are notorious for rooting through litter boxes with some disgusting consequences—eating dirty cat litter and even feces. The result will not only be a mess but, often, a dog with an upset stomach.

If your cat is willing to use a covered litter box, that can solve the problem, Weigner points out. But if your cat will only use the open kind, place the litter box in a space (like a bathroom or laundry room) with a child gate in the doorway so the cat, but not the dog, can get through. A dog-free zone will give your cat relief from canine-caused stress and protect your pup's health, too.

not trying to injure each other," Weigner says. "I rarely see a cat injured by another cat. The fighting is more bluster than anything else. One cat will fluff up and hiss and scream and hope the other will back off—but usually they aren't even using their claws."

Weigner recommends that cat owners use a diffuser to dispense synthesized versions of feline pheromones, which are produced by glands in cat whiskers (and humans can't smell them). When you see cats rubbing the side of their face against their owner's leg or furniture, they are marking their territory with the pheromones. Using the synthesized version in your home for about a month exerts a calming effect on the cats and reduces the territorial fighting.

"It's not a panacea and it doesn't sedate your cat—I don't recommend sedatives or other drugs—but the pheromones clearly help calm the situation," explains Weigner.

To introduce a new cat to your current feline, consider these steps:
• When the new cat first comes into the household, keep the kitties separate for a day with their own water, food and litter box. If they can smell each other at the bottom of the door, that's fine.
• Let them have their separate spaces for a day or two and then switch areas—put your established kitty into the room where you've been keeping the new cat and let the new cat walk around the house for a few hours.

A quarter of all U.S. households own at least one cat, with an average of 1.8 per home, according to the American Veterinary Medical Association.

A cat will first show dominance with body language.

Cats sometimes display defensive aggression when they feel threatened.

• Then open the door and let them discover each other again. They will probably act like they hate each other, although rarely, two cats will quickly decide they love each other. More likely, there will be some noise and you will think they are going to kill each other. The fight will typically only last a few seconds, though it may seem more like hours to the owner, according to Weigner.

• Never put your hands in the middle of a catfight. If you feel you must do something to break it up, spray the cats with water pistols or throw a pillow at them.

• Be prepared: The cats may fight again a second and third time, but they usually do it less and less, Weigner emphasizes. And, almost always—99 percent of the time—the cats will work it out and soon be sharing the house in peace and purrs. It's tempting to provide your only cat with a feline or canine friend, and animal behaviorists suggest you fulfill this urge for the health and happiness of your cat. After all, a cat alone suffers from boredom and lacks a natural social milieu. Just make sure you follow the guidelines laid out here to keep your kitty safe. 🐾

When adding a dog to a family with cats, consult a canine behaviorist about the best breed.

To successfully launch your interspecies family, make sure that you adopt a kitten before adding a puppy to the mix.

Cats and dogs can sleep together, share the same water bowl and even groom each other.

CREATING THE *PURRFECT* MUSIC

Finding tunes your feline will love.

Your kitten won't respond to human music, but composer and cellist David Teie aims to give the joy of music to cats by taking the feline brain into account. He launched his effort to create music for other species with cotton-top tamarin monkeys, who "showed little interest in human music" but were excited by Teie's enlivening melodies and relaxed by his calming compositions.

Next, he began composing for the domestic cat. "Cats were widely kept as pets, allowing us to easily share music with them," Teie explains. Teie's efforts have long been studied by psychologists Charles Snowden and Megan Savage, whose work has been published in major scientific journals. A Kickstarter campaign raised enough money to produce CDs and digital downloads, now available at musicforcats.com. Here, he shares insights into his work.

Keyboard Cat,
look out: There's
more music you may
enjoy hearing.

How did you study the connection between music and emotion?

First, I took music apart, breaking it into indivisible elements. An example of such an element is pulse, a feature present in the music of all cultures. Then I asked the question of each element: Why would this affect human emotions? After a few years of investigation, I had plausible answers for about 26 different elements of music.

So you decided to test your theory by writing music for nonhuman species?

Yes. Basically, animals don't give a hoot for our music but they respond when the basic elements are changed for them. Based on that, I wrote music for cotton-top tamarin monkeys that was tested by psychologist Charles Snowdon. With his colleague Megan Savage, he then tested the effect of my music for cats and published the results in *Applied Animal Behavior Science* in 2015. The data on the cats was even stronger than the monkey data.

Can you give an example of how it works?

The pulse in our music is based on the pulse we all heard in the womb. The brain structures responsible for emotions are almost completely formed at birth, and the fetus has been listening to the loud sounds (72 decibels!) of the womb for five months. But the brain of a cat is an eighth the size at birth that it will be at 10 weeks, so most of the brain development happens outside the womb. I figured that a reward-related sound all cats would experience as their brains develop is the sound of suckling. As a result, the pulse in music for cats is more like a quick whishing sound.

Are there special tools or software needed to make music for cats?

A good deal of software was required to modify the recorded acoustic instruments in order to create [music for cats]. As you can imagine, human music had lots of time and people to develop instruments. My favorite purr instrument required the combination of three sounds and instruments (including drumming on a toy football); five people (including the percussionist, recording engineer and sound designer); and four software programs to create a single 2-second purr "instrument."

Would this kind of music work on all cats?

I'm sure everything would need to be different for the big cats. The suckling sounds would be similar, although slower. Of the big cats, I understand that only the cheetah purrs, and that purr is a bit slower than the domestic cat's, so I believe it could be modified for the cheetah. Providing enrichment for captive species is a primary goal of mine.

What about music for other species?

I had a failure in my test of music through headphones for horses. There was no response to the music. I think it was too soft and distant from the tympanic membrane to make any difference, and the headphones came off. Dogs are challenging, due to the variety of sizes in breeds and their connection to humans.

What are your greatest challenges?

Trying to think like a cat, hear as a cat hears and invent instruments based on natural and acoustic sounds. ✿

> Animals are known to respond to music when some of the basic elements are rearranged to better suit their tastes.

About 3.2 million cats
are brought to shelters
in the U.S. each year.

SAVED

HOW TO RESCUE A CAT

Pet cats can get lost or, tragically, dumped on the streets by heartless or financially strapped owners. These animals need a hero—and that hero could be you.

One morning near the end of January, I found myself driving home around 8 a.m. with the windows down and my eyes watering. Sure, it was freezing, but I didn't have a better option: Beside me in the passenger seat rested a cat carrier, holding a very frightened and viciously malodorous stray kitty.

Here's how it happened: This guy Paul, who works with my wife, had been feeding a stray cat who'd been hanging around near his house. He'd been doing this for a few months, but with winter settling in, he worried about how the cat would survive.

My wife and I have rescued a few cats in our time, so she told him that if he captured the cat, we'd take it from there. He called a few nights later to tell us he'd done it, and we set up a cat handoff for the next day.

I could tell something hadn't gone so well when I got close to Paul's car. The window was down, and a foul odor wafted out. Paul looked ill.

"He didn't like being stuck in the carrier," Paul said.

Really didn't like it. The poor cat had gone bonkers once the carrier door was shut—hissed and spat and scrabbled frantically at every crack. Paul managed to push some food and water into the carrier, but he

and water into the carrier, but he couldn't let the cat out for the night because he didn't think he'd ever get him back in there.

He put the carrier in his basement, where he'd hoped the darkness and quiet would help the cat calm down. But it made no difference. The kitty had spent the night in such a spasm of terror that he'd peed and pooped all over himself. On top of that, he exuded a rank, almost skunky pheromonal fear odor. The desperate little guy was hunkered down in the carrier now, too exhausted to struggle, and stinking like nothing I had ever encountered.

There wasn't anything else to be done. I put the carrier into my car, shook Paul's hand, and started the 45-minute drive home.

FRIENDLY OR FERAL?

Paul was lucky—he had help available via my wife. But what if you don't have someone like us to call? The first thing to do when you find a feline wandering outdoors is determine what sort of cat you're dealing with. Is it domesticated (a house cat) or feral (wild)? Is it a neighbor's cat looking for an extra meal, or a genuinely lost pet? What you should do depends entirely on the answers to these questions.

Not every cat living outside is lost or abandoned. Feral cats, who have never been pets and live like raccoons and possums and other wild animals, roam the alleyways of cities and the fields of the countryside. Such cats can benefit from human care, particularly spaying and neutering, and they'll appreciate feeding—but you definitely shouldn't try to rescue them. They don't want to become pets or live in houses. They don't *need* to be rescued.

Distinguishing a stray house cat from a feral cat isn't always easy, though there are some clear indicators. A cat that has been "ear-tipped," for example, is almost certainly feral. Look for one ear, usually the left, that's cleanly squared-off rather than pointy. (A quick web search will turn up plenty of example photos.) This mark indicates that a feral cat has been trapped before and spayed or neutered. It prevents those who work with feral cat colonies from retrapping cats unnecessarily.

A cat that's friendly and comfortable around people, on the other hand, is definitely domesticated. "If it comes and rubs on your leg or meows at you, it's a house cat," says Jessica Gotthold, CEO of The National Foundation for Animal Rescue.

Some lost or stray domesticated cats, however, won't be that comfortable with you right away. If they've been living outside for a while, they may have become more cautious and fearful of humans, even if they're still struggling to survive on their own. "Sit outside with them, even if you can't touch them," says Doreen Kaminski, a longtime volunteer with Whiskers Pet Rescue in Southbury, Connecticut. "Bring food out, earn their trust."

Some pets are cruelly abandoned to fend for themselves, but there's just as good a chance that a nonferal cat you find hanging around your yard has an owner somewhere who would like to see her come home. Offer food, if she seems hungry. Take her to a vet, if she's obviously sick or injured. But use caution: Get someone to help if the cat tries to scratch or bite.

After you have attended to the cat's essential needs, try to locate the owner, if you can. If someone comes forward claiming the cat, however, be careful. Leave some important information out of your description of the cat, a distinguishing detail such as a missing tooth, extra toes or that odd orange spot.

> If a lost and frightened cat is hard to approach, sit outside with her and bring her milk and food to earn her trust.

Not all cats want to be "rescued." Feral ones do much better in the wild.

Pet cats are increasingly likely to have microchips that identify their human owners.

Need a Good Home!

If you want to add a cat to your family, turn to local shelters before going to a commercial breeder.

Rescue shelters and humane societies can help you find the perfect pet kitten or cat.

FIVE WAYS TO FIND THE OWNER OF A LOST CAT

If you're feeding a stray cat or you've rescued a kitty from the risky outdoors, try to find the cat's missing family by following these important steps.

1 Ask Around Your Neighborhood

This may be a cat that lives nearby but likes to wander in search of extra food or attention. Check with as many people as you can— and make sure to go at least a couple of blocks beyond your street in each direction. (A photograph of the cat will help eliminate the uncertainty that comes with relying on a verbal description.) If you come across the owner or a neighbor that knows the cat and where it lives, you're all set— your work is done.

2 Check the Chip

If the cat is approachable enough to catch, then you may be in luck. Pet cats are increasingly likely to have microchips—tiny transponders embedded just under the skin— and just about any veterinarian or shelter will be able to check for a chip in less than a minute. Find a chip, and bingo! You'll have the name, address and phone number of the cat's owner. Caroline Abate, director of Whiskers Pet Rescue, recalls one recent case of a cat that hopped into a UPS delivery truck and ended up 40 miles from home. "It took about two months," she says, "but eventually we did get the cat home."

3 Talk to Vets, Shelters and Animal Control

People looking for lost pets often contact nearby veterinarians, shelters and animal-control offices, so these places may have heard from the owner of the cat you've found. (Note that, in some areas, you might be legally required to report finding a cat to your local city or town animal shelter, so be sure to check your local laws.)

4 Create a Flyer

If you still have no leads on an owner, make a simple flyer you can post around the area. Include your phone number, a photo of the cat and a simple description.

5 Use Social Media and Lost-Pet Websites

The internet offers lots of ways to spread the word about a lost cat. Look for lost-cat postings from around your area and post information about the cat you found.

You should use the information that you withheld to screen any claimants. Unfortunately, some people will claim animals that aren't theirs to sell or use for awful purposes, so check everyone out. Ask for their vet's name and call the office to verify. Get their full name, address and phone number—and

Travel carriers are convenient for transporting sick or rescued cats to the vet.

check it against their ID. This may seem paranoid, but it's important. You don't want to turn a lost kitty over to the wrong person, especially if the individual is abusive.

STEPPING UP

If you are lucky enough to find a lost cat's owner, the search might still take weeks. In the meantime, the cat will be your temporary charge.

If the weather is harsh and cold, you'll want to find a way to provide some shelter. With a friendly cat, you've got the option of taking it into your house or setting it up with a warm bed in your garage (if you have one). Especially if you don't have any other pets, this may be the way to go.

With a less-approachable kitty, you may want to consider building a little shelter that can sit in your yard. This doesn't have to be a lot of work; you can find instructions for various designs with a Google search, and many shelter and rescue groups will happily offer advice.

In warmer seasons or climes, shelter from the elements isn't such a worry—but the cat still may be in danger staying outside. Coyotes and other predators pose a threat in rural and many suburban settings. Road traffic is always a peril. Or maybe someone else in the neighborhood doesn't like having stray cats around and will turn to poison or a hunting rifle to solve the problem.

You'll have to assess the situation as best you can and decide how urgent it is to bring the cat inside while you look for its rightful home. If you can't take the cat in, you may decide to bring it to a shelter for safety. Call first to see if the shelter has space for a new cat—and make sure it has a no-kill policy.

Let's say you've tried everything, and it's been several weeks without any sign of an owner coming forward to claim the cat. At this point, you must weigh options for the future.

If you can provide a good home for the cat yourself, that would be best for everyone. The cat already knows you, if you've been feeding and interacting with it. He or she will be more comfortable with you than with someone brand-new.

If you can't adopt the cat yourself, maybe you know someone who can. Talk to friends, relatives and neighbors to see if they might be interested. Feel free to nudge them a bit—this kitty needs a home, and sometimes people need a little

> **If you can't find a stray's owner after several weeks, it may be time for you to step up and adopt the cat yourself.**

encouragement—but don't push too hard. You don't want to place the cat with someone who won't care for it well, and you don't want someone to resent you for placing a burden on them that they're truly not ready for. If possible, offer to make the placement on a trial basis, promising to take the cat back and look for another adopter, if things aren't working out.

CAT HOTEL

If you can't care for the cat and have found no one else who can, you may need to contact a shelter once more for help. Wherever you live, there are probably several nearby organizations that run shelters, provide foster homes and seek adopters for homeless cats. A simple internet search should bring up options. (Petfinder.com also has a searchable list of shelters and rescues around the country.) Again, make sure that the organization you contact won't euthanize the animal. You're trying to rescue the cat, not get it killed. And bear in mind that these groups are under a lot of pressure. They've got limited resources and far more needy cats than they can handle.

"We try to help as much as possible," says rescue volunteer Kaminski, "but we do get full."

Be flexible and "work with the organization," says cat-rescue activist Caroline Abate. "If you can provide food and shelter for a few days, put the cat in your garage or in a bathroom—that will buy the rescuers some time" to find space for the cat. Most important, don't give up. It may take awhile to find a group that has the time and space to help, but persistence will lead to an answer.

If you have no other choice—either by law or circumstance—but to turn the cat over to your local animal-control center, at least ask about their policies.

You may get lucky: Many municipal shelters won't kill animals or will at least wait several weeks before putting them down. "There's a lot less euthanasia going on than 15 or 20 years ago," says Mike Rueb, who is operations manager at The National Cat Protection Society. "There's more of a push these days to give the animals that come in a real chance."

But that's far from universal. If the cat might be euthanized, consider putting your name in as a last-ditch adopter who is willing to take the cat in before it is put to death. And call often to check on the cat so that the shelter knows someone cares.

This may sound like an awful lot to think about. You probably didn't think that helping a stray cat could be so complicated! Rescuing cats certainly isn't the easiest way to spend an afternoon—it requires patience and perseverance, kindness and care. But it's also enormously rewarding. You're saving a life. So watch out—the first cat you rescue probably won't be your last. —*Robert K. J. Killheffer* 🐾

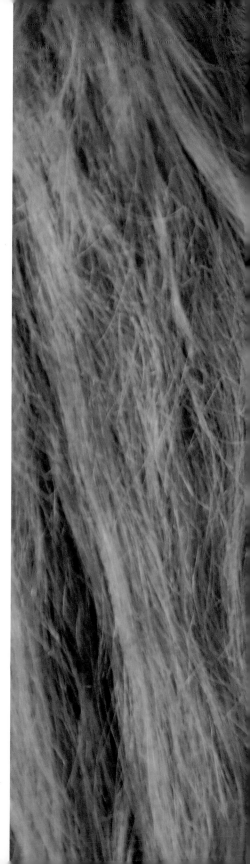

Some cats do better without competition from other household pets.

Saving a cat is complicated, but when you rescue a cat, you are saving a life.

LONGEVITY

CARING FOR AN AGING CAT

Cats were once considered seniors at age 8—but today,
many live into their late teens and early 20s.
Here's how to help them make the most of their golden years.

Cats rely on us to care for them throughout their lives. But they need us the most when they're very young and again when they're old. At age 12, a cat is 64 in people years. He can live well beyond that with the right diet, exercise, veterinary care and attention from you.

The right care is especially critical today, when cats tend to live into their teens or 20s, three times longer than in the past. To care for your senior cat, watch for signs of aging, from lack of balance to brittle claws and thicker pads on paws. Jumping up on the sofa could prove difficult. Aging cats can miss the litter box when urinating, and you might notice loss of luster in her coat or a few gray hairs.

"Older cats experience a decline in their ability to hear subtle noises, and may lose some visual sharpness," says Robin Downing, DVM, of The Downing Center for Animal Pain Management in Windsor, Colorado. "This shrinks their world and can have a detrimental effect on their mental health."

To protect your aging cat from harm, stay alert to small problems before they become big. Addressing health issues at the initial stage makes for a better outcome than letting the illness progress.

WATCH FOR PROBLEMS AND INTERVENE EARLY

Look for subtle problems first. With aging and illness, you need to be aware of any changes in your cat's behavior and appearance, or you'll miss something that could be treated before the problem becomes worse. Is your cat sleeping more than usual? Sometimes it's hard to tell, since most cats sleep between 12 and 16 hours a day. Maybe he doesn't come when you call. He might be hiding. Look for clues and start with those that are more obvious.

Weight loss and weight gain are easy to detect. The pounds might drop due to dental disease, which makes it painful to eat. According to the College of Veterinary Medicine at Cornell University, an estimated 85 percent of cats over the age of 6 suffer from some form of periodontal disease. The good news is it's preventable, with semiannual trips to the veterinarian.

Other forms of weight loss can be caused by disease of the kidneys, thyroid, liver or heart, all illnesses more common in older cats.

The opposite health problem for cats is obesity. According to the Association for Pet Obesity and Prevention, almost 60 percent of cats in the U.S. are overweight or obese. Cats that are carrying extra fat are at greater risk for developing diabetes, arthritis, high blood pressure, kidney disease and many forms of cancer than leaner kitties. All these illnesses can shorten your cat's life.

Exercise, diet, dental care and abundant play will all help extend your senior cat's life.

An aging cat needs an extra dose of care, love and attention.

167

Exercise, diet and portion control play major roles in keeping your cat healthy longer. A veterinarian can guide you on weight-loss options that benefit your cat, starting when she is young. Addressing health issues earlier makes for a better outcome later on.

PROTECT YOUR PET'S BRAIN

Aging cats can develop signs of senility. "As cats get older," Amy Shojai writes in her book *Complete Care for Your Aging Cat*, "the blood flow to the brain is reduced, causing a loss of neurons the body is unable to replace." Indeed, some 30 percent of older cats show changes in behavior—and in cats over 16 years of age, that number increases to almost 90 percent.

Senior cats, like humans, can develop flagrant dementia—a condition called cognitive dysfunction syndrome, or CDS; it is marked by amyloid plaque, much like Alzheimer's. They might suddenly become terrified at being left alone; might forget how to use the litter box; and might not even recognize old friends. The cat with dementia can lose track of normal sleep and wake patterns and may become especially noisy through the night. They may also demonstrate obsessive and compulsive behaviors similar to obsessive-compulsive disorder (OCD).

But as in the case with an elderly Alzheimer's patient, cats with dementia can be helped. One

If your cat sleeps on your bed, place carpet-covered steps next to it for access.

Older cats may spend much of the day sleeping but still be playful when awake.

possible avenue for slowing down symptoms is nutrition. "Dietary management with vegetables, nuts, whole grains and vitamins E and C can reduce the risk of cognitive decline and dementia in humans, and various dietary products containing anti-oxidants, fish oils and other nutritional supplements are promoted for use in cats with age-related problems" as well, according to veterinarians Christos Karagiannis and Professor Daniel Mills of the University of Lincoln in the United Kingdom.

In one study of 46 cats, a diet supplemented with nutrients including tocopherols, L-carnitine, vitamin C, beta-carotene, docosahexaenoic acid, methionine and cysteine appeared to result in improvement of symptoms—but who could say which of the many ingredients was effective? Another supplement containing choline, phosphatidylcholine, methionine, inositol, vitamin E, zinc, selenium, taurine and other B vitamins, meanwhile, seemed to reduce confusion and improve appetite in nine out of 21 cats.

The most effective therapy, however, is still personal. On the most basic level, make sure that you interact and play with your cat in order to keep her brain stimulated. Puzzles and games for your older cat should be abundant.

You need to keep activity alive, but not over-the-top. For instance, say Karagiannis and Mills, don't bring a lively new kitten into the house to perk up your senior cat—that will only increase his anxiety. And don't expect your senior cat to play rough-and-tumble games, as in the past. Alternative activities, like hide-and-seek or reward-based training and new forms of object play —for instance, hanging toys—can provide useful mental stimulation, the veterinarians say.

PAY ATTENTION TO CUDDLE TIME

In sum, your aging cat needs your emotional presence more than ever. "While cats may create the impression they can live without us," says Downing, "they are actually very social creatures, enjoying their time with us. They're not as active as they once were, but they do enjoy being the focus of your attention. The bonus is that interacting with your senior cat will keep him healthier and more alert—and can extend his life. Science has revealed that while stroking cats can reduce our heart rates and blood pressure, that interaction also does the same for the cat."

Older cats don't get into everything, like they once did when they were kittens. Now is the time to enjoy those quiet times. "Seek out your older cat when you get ready to sit down at your computer or to watch TV or read a book," Downing says. "These are times that they will often enjoy sitting near you or on your lap." ❧

Mature cats can be a comfort to elderly humans.

As your cat ages, you might notice a few gray hairs in the whiskers and coat.

171

HELPING YOUR CAT THRIVE

Playing with their human companions keeps cats from getting bored and indulging in destructive behavior.

CATS JUST WANT TO HAVE FUN

Talking, playing and spending time with your furry friends
promotes good health, busts boredom and makes for happy kitties.

173

Cats can have a blast indoors. Not only do they live three to four times longer than their outdoor-only counterparts, their stalking instinct can be stimulated from the safety and comfort of your home.

"Enrichment is the key to keeping cats from getting bored," says Samantha Bell, cat behavior and enrichment lead for Best Friends Animal Society in Los Angeles. "And the No. 1 form of cat enrichment is interactive playtime. Cats are predators at their core, and all cats feel their happiest and most confident when they feel like they're 'killing' their prey." According to Bell, "you can help your cats feel the thrill of the hunt by enriching all five senses and giving them things a wild cat would enjoy. Try to bring the outdoors inside by letting them see the birds outside, smell catnip, taste new and exciting meat treats, hear birds or rodents, and touch novel surfaces like cat grass and different types of scratchers."

You can place a sofa, a large comfy chair or a perch for your cats by a window so they can watch the birds from the safety of your living room. Play online videos or turn your television to a wildlife channel so your cats can listen to the chirps and chattering sounds of prey.

"One way to help your cats feel like the fierce predator they were born to be is by engaging in interactive playtime," Bell says. "Some cats love to chase after wand toys with a mouse on the end that you drag and make scurry along the ground. Some prefer to fly through the air, jumping for a wand toy with feathers on the end."

Playtime can vary from two or more 10- to 15-minute play sessions each day. This will improve your cat's health by keeping him engaged, fit and trim. Overweight couch-potato cats can suffer from health problems.

In fact, you can be the antidote for your cat's obesity, an increasingly dangerous problem for the sedentary and overfed domestic feline, afflicting some 59 percent of cats overall. This excess weight increases the risk of arthritis, diabetes, heart and respiratory disease, kidney disease and cancer. Because your cat is especially motivated to play with you, however, you can encourage active play sessions and romps around the house; these should be scheduled a couple of times a day.

Remember, a bored cat can be a destructive cat. With nothing to do, scratching the furniture or climbing on the curtains can be fun to a bored kitty. To discourage this negative behavior and to promote fun, Bell suggests training your cat. "Engaging them in positive, reward-based training, like clicker-training," Bell says, "promotes good behaviors. Cats are extremely trainable, and it's a great way to bond with your cat."

What if your cat doesn't respond to any of this? Experts advise that you rule out illness with a visit to the vet. Once he has a clean bill of health, redouble your efforts to keep your furry friend amused.

A good view can be entertaining to a house cat waiting for the family to come home.

All cats, even this sweet orange tabby, are natural predators.

Keep Your Cat Engaged

1 Adopt a second cat to keep your cat from getting bored. Make sure they're compatible.

2 Schedule two daily 15-minute play sessions with your cat. You can do this in the morning before you go to work and in the evening when you're home. Increase the time together on the weekends.

3 Many cats love chasing laser pointers. Just make sure not to shine the light into their eyes. It could harm them.

4 Rotate their toys. Just as you would do with kids' toys, put away some of your cat's toys so he's playing with one at a time.

5 Treat your cat to catnip toys. This plant is thought to trigger cat pheromones, and is safe for your kitties.

6 Make your own cat toys. Take an old sock and fill it with catnip or a ball.

7 Most cats love cardboard boxes and brown paper bags. Remove the handles, then leave them out so your cat can play in them.

8 Place scratching posts around the house. Find something sturdy and tall enough so your cat can stretch out while scratching.

9 Get a cat tower with a scratching post so your cat can climb, scratch and play. This will keep your cat busy (and keep him from ruining the sofa). 🐾

THE CAT IN THE BOX

It's not what's inside the package that counts.

Cats cannot resist boxes. When I get a package in the mail, my cat waits for me to unpack it and then immediately dives in. Sometimes she naps, sometimes she picks at the cardboard with her claws, but most of the time she just sits there contentedly. Such behavior is universal among cats—even among big ones. YouTube videos show lions, bobcats, leopards, tigers and other predatory felines playing with and lounging in massive cardboard boxes. Is box love in cats' DNA?

Cats can get stressed and anxious. While cats have evolved to manage lifestyle stresses (like humans, their hormones and nervous system elicit a fight-or-flight response), long-term stress associated with domestication or humans can be more difficult. Cats can get stressed if they lack proper food, water or litter boxes—or if they live with other cats, dogs, toddlers or owners who insist on more socializing than the cat seems to desire.

Research also suggests that cats are sensitive to their owners' stress levels, so that bad day you had at work could also affect your feline. Just as with humans, stress affects not only a cat's behavior but also its physical health.

When cats get stressed or anxious, they hide. Research conducted by Dutch veterinary medicine professors found that access to boxes reduced stress in shelter cats. The cats with access to boxes adjusted to a level of "recovery" after two days, while the cats without boxes didn't attain a similar level of adjustment until two weeks had passed.

Boxes also offer warmth. A National Research Council study found that domestic cats prefer temperatures between 86°F and 97°F because they don't have to expend energy to warm or cool themselves. Curling up inside a cardboard box allows cats to generate and maintain heat, which adds to the cozy, secure feeling. Maybe that explains why cats enjoy stuffing themselves into boxes half their size?

Keeping a box or two around is an easy way to get your cat to take the equivalent of a few deep breaths. If you move, have a baby, adopt another pet or have a situation that might result in stress for your cat, putting out an extra box or two might help—and it's cheaper than therapy.—*Joelle Renstrom* ❧

> ## Cats are known to hide during times of stress, so having a box on hand can keep them from getting anxious or needy.

Who knew a simple cardboard box could be so entertaining?

10 AMAZING FELINE FACTS

Think you know all there is to know about your furry friend?
Some of these fascinating bits may surprise you!

1 **Cats don't have a sweet tooth.** If your cat eats ice cream, it's not because it's sweet. Your cat can't actually taste sugar; it's because he's drawn to the fat, according to the *Journal of Nutrition*. Humans have five different receptors—salty, bitter, sour, savory and sweet—but cats lack the sweet receptor.

2

Cats are nearsighted. Despite the fact that cats' peripheral and night visions are better than ours, they can't see objects that are far away like we do, according to veterinarian Lynn Buzhardt of Veterinary Centers of America. "If a human sees an object clearly from a distance of 100 feet, it will appear blurry to a cat," she says.

3

Cats walk like camels and giraffes. Watch your cat walk: He'll move both of his right feet first, then his left. Cats, camels and giraffes are the only four-legged animals to walk this way. All others start with the left front leg at the same time as the right hind leg, then their right front leg with their left hind leg.

4 Cats love carbs. Cats are supposed to be the ultimate carnivores, but in a recent study from Oregon State University, researchers found that, when given a choice, cats consumed most of their calories in carbs—as opposed to dogs, who gravitated to fat. Based on food intake calculations over 28 days, the researchers' report in the *Journal of Experimental Biology* says dogs on average chose to consume most of their calories from fat (about 41 percent) and then carbs (about 36 percent), whereas cats on average chose to consume most of their calories from carbs (43 percent) and then protein (about 30 percent) Protein intake was also influenced by body mass and age. Younger, leaner cats consumed more protein compared with older cats, who had moderate protein intake and lower circulating concentrations of DHA, an omega-3 fatty acid associated with heart and brain health.

5 Cats can be left- or right-pawed. A study at the Animal Behavior Centre at Queen's University Belfast found male cats tend to use their left paws more dominantly and females use their right. Of particular interest: The researchers found a sex split in the direction—although not the strength—of the cats' paw bias when reaching for food or stepping down or over things. Males showed a significant preference for using their left paw on these measures, while females were more inclined to use the right one.

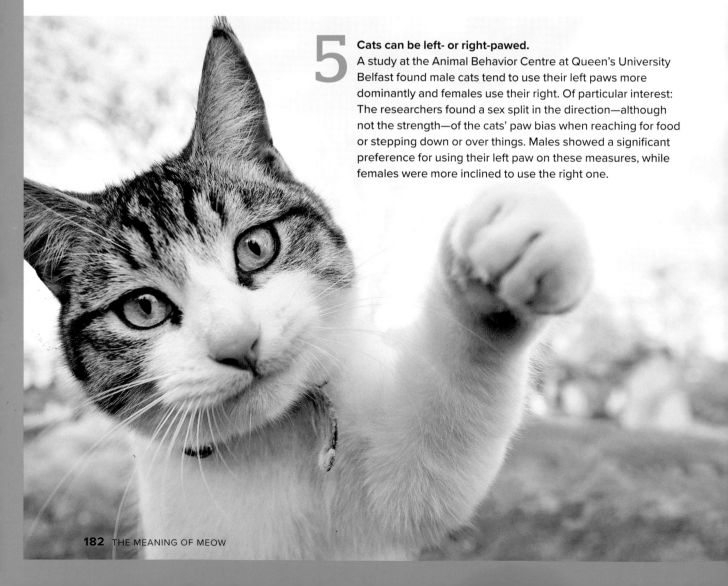

6

Cats' rough tongues can remove all shreds of meat off a bone. Researchers at Georgia Tech found that a cat's tongue surface looks like hooks in the shape of a cat's claw. Tongues from cats, bobcats, cougars, lions and tigers all revealed that these hooks, called papillae contain hollow scoops and that the papillae were only slightly larger in lions than in the average cat.

7 **Groups of cats have many different names.** Everyone knows that a group of kittens is commonly called a litter, but there are names for a pack of adult cats, too. Among them: a clowder, a clutter, a cluster, a glaring and a pounce. A cat community has also been called a kindle or an intrigue. Intrigue makes perfect sense because it's defined as a mysterious or fascinating quality.

8 **Cats are living longer, and spaying and neutering helps.** Great news! According to a study from NYC's Banfield Pet Hospital, a cat's average life span is on the upswing, and fertility control helps. Neutered male cats live 62 percent longer than unneutered males, and spayed female cats live 37 percent longer than unspayed females. Neutering male pets decreases their chances of developing prostatic enlargement and disease and eliminates the risk of testicular cancer, the hospital says, while spaying female pets eliminates the risk of pyometra, a life-threatening infection of the uterus. If a female is spayed before her first heat cycle, the chances of her developing breast cancer drop dramatically as well.

9 **In the perennial contest between dog versus cat brainpower, dogs win by a head.** Researchers from Vanderbilt University have finally completed their count of neurons in brains of carnivores, including cats and dogs. "In this study, we were interested in comparing different species," said biologist Suzana Herculano-Houzel. The scientists looked at neurons in the cerebral cortex associated with planning, thinking, complex behavior and overall intelligence. The tally: About 250 million cortical neurons for cats and 530 million for dogs—as opposed to some 16 billion in the human brain.

10 **In the cat versus rat war, the rats are winning.** A study published in *Frontiers in Ecology and Evolution* in 2018 reports that cats are ineffective at controlling populations of rats. Indeed, when we release cats into the wild, they may be more visible than rats to our human eyes, but the impression is illusory. "For every additional cat sighting, a rat is 1.19 times more likely to move in the direction of shelter," the researchers say. Their findings support recent objections to releasing cats, who prey on many species aside from rats. "Even though rats were less likely to be seen in the areas the scientists studied, they still remained present in the system."

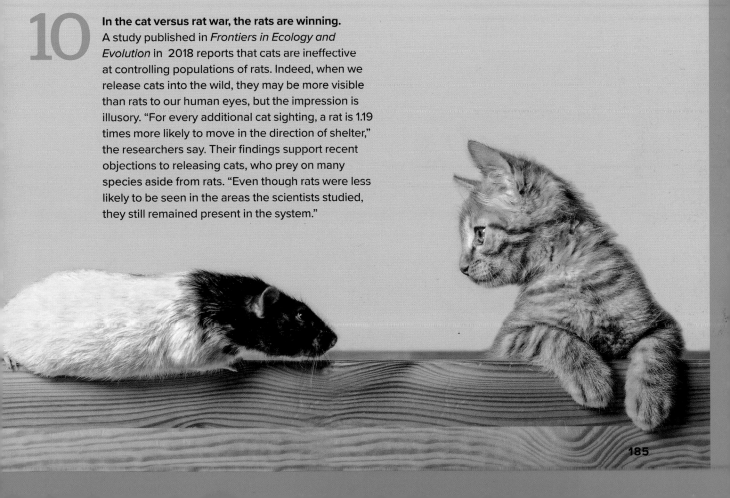

CREDITS

COVER Sonsedska Yuliia/Shutterstock FRONT FLAP Allison Achauer/Getty Images 1 Sonsedska Yuliia/Shutterstock 2-3 Purple Collar Pet Photography/Getty Images 4-5 (From left) HollenderX2/Getty Images; hocus-focus/Getty Images; Elles Rijsdijk/EyeEm/ Getty Images; Allison Achauer/Getty Images; Agency Animal Picture/Getty Images 6-7 skynesher/Getty Images 8 Agency Animal Picture/Getty Images 9 Chase Dekker Wild-Life Images/Getty Images 10 Elles Rijsdijk/EyeEm/Getty Images 11 Frédéric Sécher/ EyeEm/Getty Images 12 Ambre Haller/Getty Images 13 Vladyslav Rybalchenko/EyeEm/Getty Images 14-15 Tara Moore/Getty Images 16 Rodolfo Parulan Jr./Getty Images 17 Francoise de Valera/Alamy Stock Photo 18-19 Image(s) by Sara Lynn Paige/Getty Images 20 Oksana Ariskina/oxygen/Getty Images 21 Natalia Ganelin/Getty Images 22-23 Africa Studio/Shutterstock 24-25 New Africa/Shutterstock 26-27 (From left) D-Keine/Getty Images; Meaghan Skinner Photography/Getty Images 28 joeyful/Getty Images 29 Image by Chris Winsor/Getty Images 30-31 Ronnachai Palas/EyeEm/Getty Images 32 Cyndi Monaghan/Getty Images 33 Dorling Kindersley ltd/Alamy Stock Photo 34 Celeste Martearena/Getty Images 35 Westend61/Getty Images 36-37 jeep2499/ Shutterstock 39 Gallo Images-Dave Hamman/Getty Images 40 Christophel Fine Art/Getty Images 41 DEA/A. DAGLI ORTI/Getty Images 42-43 Martyn Hayes/Getty Images 44-45 Susanne Hegbart/EyeEm/Getty Images 46 graphixel/Getty Images 47 (From top) Courtesy Edward Lowe Foundation; perets/Getty Images 48 sylvia born/Alamy Stock Photo 49 Lina Keil/Shutterstock 50-51 LightFieldStudios/Getty Images 52-53 CasarsaGuru/Getty Images 54-55 imageBROKER/Alamy Stock Photo 56-57 RooM the Agency/Alamy Stock Photo 58 www.sharp-photo.com/Getty Images 59-60 Life On White/Getty Images (2) 61 Fabio Petroni/ Getty Images 62 Agency Animal Picture/Getty Images 63 adisa/iStockphoto 64 VladislavStarozhilov/iStockphoto 65 Animal Photography/Alamy Stock Photo 66 Utekhina Anna/Shutterstock 67 dien/Shutterstock 68 Luis Alvarez/Getty Images 69 (From left) Eric Isselee/Shutterstock; Evdoha_spb/Shutterstock 70 (From left) Just-Mila/Shutterstock; GlobalP/iStockphoto 71 (From left) Eric Isselee/Shutterstock; By Wunderfool/Getty Images 72 (From top) fotojagodka/iStockphoto; Arco Images GmbH/Alamy Stock Photo 73 (From left) hocus-focus/Getty Images; DenisNata/Shutterstock 74 (From top) Eric Isselee/Shutterstock; Nailia Schwarz/ Shutterstock 75 (From left) GlobalP/iStockphoto; Sergey Skleznev/iStockphoto 76-77 sdominick/Getty Images 78-79 Malcolm MacGregor/Getty Images 80-81 marieclaudelemay/Getty Images 82-83 Africa Studio/Shutterstock 84-85 Hero Images/Getty Images 86-87 gradyreese/Getty Images 89 Waitforlight/Getty Images 90-91 Toshiro Shimada/Getty Images 92-93 yoyoshot/Getty Images 94 (From left) Zhalabkovich Yauheniya/Shutterstock; Susan Schmitz/Shutterstock; Nils Jacobi/Getty Images 95 Yulia-Images/Getty Images 96-97 Peresmeh/Getty Images 98 Ryan McVay/Getty Images 99 (From left) Life On White/Getty Images; Mary Swift/Shutterstock 100-101 Evgenia Terehova/Shutterstock 102-103 Lopolo/Shutterstock 104-105 Olya Detry/Shutterstock 106-107 ¬© by Martin Deja/Getty Images 108-109 namussi/Getty Images 110-111 NomadicImagery/Getty Images 113 Akimasa Harada/Getty Images 114-115 ICHAUVEL/Getty Images 116-117 Strela Studio/Shutterstock 118-119 Juniors Bildarchiv GmbH/Alamy Stock Photo 120-121 (From left) Tierfotoagentur/Alamy Stock Photo; Carrie Anne Castillo/Getty Images 123 Tierfotoagentur/Alamy Stock Photo 124-125 Juniors Bildarchiv GmbH/Alamy Stock Photo 126-127 Carlina Teteris/Getty Images 128-129 Waitforlight/ Getty Images 131 Vasilyev Alexandr/Shutterstock 132 Johner Images/Getty Images 133 Benjamin Torode/Getty Images 134 Allison Achauer/Getty Images 135 Kacy Kizer/Getty Images 137 Ittipol Nampochai/EyeEm/Getty Images 139 Irina Kozorog/ Shutterstock 141 Chendongshan/Shutterstock 142 Grigorita Ko/Shutterstock 145 Carlos G. Lopez/Getty Images 146-147 cynoclub/ Getty Images 148-149 Gladskikh Tatiana/Shutterstock 150-151 Kristina Kohanova/EyeEm/Getty Images 152 Belozerova Daria/ Alamy Stock Photo 154-155 Vasiliki Varvaki/Getty Images 157 Andrei Troitskiy/Getty Images 158-159 Thinkstock/Getty Images 160-161 frantic00/Shutterstock 162-163 Africa Studio/Shutterstock 164-165 Jaromir Chalabala/EyeEm/Getty Images 166-167 Nils Jacobi/Getty Images 168-169 Daniel Levick/EyeEm/Getty Images 170-171 evrymmnt/Shutterstock 172-173 CasarsaGuru/Getty Images 174-175 Westend61/Getty Images 176-177 Neil Petersen/EyeEm/Getty Images 179 A. Aleksandravicius/Getty Images 180 Nic_Ol/Getty Images 181 (From top) anniepaddington/Getty Images; Axel Bueckert/EyeEm/Getty Images 182 D.R. Hutchinson/ Getty Images 183 Westend61/Getty Images 184 bouhaous/Getty Images 185 Lightspruch/Alamy Stock Photo SPINE Ryan McVay/ Getty Images BACK FLAP Faba-Photograhpy/Getty Images BACK COVER Allison Achauer/Getty Images

SPECIAL THANKS TO CONTRIBUTING WRITERS

Sherry Baker, Michele C. Hollow, Robert K. J. Killheffer, Katka Lapelosova, Joelle Renstrom, Anita and Allen Salzberg, Jason Teich, Rosie Wolf Williams

CENTENNIAL BOOKS

An Imprint of
Centennial Media, LLC
40 Worth St., 10th Floor
New York, NY 10013, U.S.A.

CENTENNIAL BOOKS is a trademark of Centennial Media, LLC

ISBN 978-1-951274-15-3
Distributed by
Simon & Schuster, Inc.
1230 Avenue of the Americas
New York, NY 10020, U.S.A.

For information about custom editions, special sales, and premium and corporate purchases, please contact Centennial Media at contact@centennialmedia.com.

Manufactured in China

Publishers & Co-Founders Ben Harris, Sebastian Raatz
Editorial Director Annabel Vered
Creative Director Jessica Power
Executive Editor Janet Giovanelli
Design Director Ben Margherita
Deputy Editor Alyssa Shaffer
Senior Art Director Laurene Chavez
Art Directors Natali Suasnavas, Joseph Ulatowski
Production Manager Paul Rodina
Production Assistant Alyssa Swiderski
Editorial Assistant Tiana Schippa